Abortion in a Changing World

VOLUME II

The Proceedings of an International Conference
Convened in Hot Springs, Virginia, November 17–20, 1968,
by the Association for the Study of Abortion

Abortion in a Changing World

VOLUME II

Edited by Robert E. Hall, M.D.

Columbia University Press
New York & London

Robert E. Hall is Associate Professor of Clinical Obstetrics and Gynecology at Columbia University College of Physicians and Surgeons. Dr. Hall is also President of the Association for the Study of Abortion.

Copyright © 1970 Association for the Study of Abortion, Inc.
International Standard Book Number 0-231-03381-8
Library of Congress Catalog Card Number 70-99219
Printed in the United States of America
9 8 7 6 5 4 3 2

PREFACE

Abortion in a Changing World, published in two volumes, documents the proceedings of an international conference on abortion assembled by the Association for the Study of Abortion at Hot Springs, Virginia, between November 17 and 20, 1968. Volume I contains the material from five plenary sessions which dealt with the ethical, medical, legal, social, and global aspects of abortion. This, Volume II, contains the record of ten separate panel sessions devoted to abortion and animation, poverty, public health, psychiatry, obstetrics, morality, mortality, constitutionality, progeny, and womankind.

The first five of these panel sessions were held simultaneously, between 8:30 and 10:00 P.M., on November 18; the second five were held on the following evening. Six to eight panelists, including a moderator and a rapporteur, were assigned to each topic. Questions were freely asked and comments made by members of the audiences, which consisted of fifteen to twenty conference participants and observers.

A stenographic record of each session was later submitted to its rapporteur and, still later, to me for editorial revision. Unfortunately, the stenographic copy was often so unintelligible that a great deal of rewriting was required. The content of significant passages was rechecked by the speakers, however, so I am confident that the basic substance of their remarks has not been disturbed.

Although I will assume the responsibility for the overall accuracy of this report, I want especially to thank the rapporteurs for their enormous help in rendering this material more readable. Additional acknowledgments and a general description of the conference will be found in the preface to Volume I.

Many, if not most, of the world's experts on abortion participated in this conference. Through this publication of their views it is their hope and mine that the subject of abortion will be more widely understood.

Robert E. Hall, M.D.
Editor

New York, New York
October 1969

CONTENTS

Contents   viii

ABORTION AND ANIMATION

The Metaphysical Conundrum
Concerning the Moment of Ensoulment

Thomas A. Wassmer, S.J., Ph.D. (moderator)
Israel R. Margolies, Ph.D. (rapporteur)
George W. Corner, M.D., LL.D.
Joseph Fletcher, S.T.D.
David Granfield, LL.B., S.T.D.
Andie L. Knutson, Ph.D.
Cyril C. Means, Jr., J.D., LL.M.
Max L. Stackhouse, Ph.D.

WASSMER: Scientists tend to agree that human life, that all life, goes back into antiquity. But when does specifically human life begin? On that question we find less agreement than did the ancient Greeks. Aristotle thought that the fetus had a soul forty days after conception. Later it was thought that ensoulment takes a longer period of time. Plato argued that life begins at birth. The Stoics thought that the fetus became animate when it breathed. Heraclitus, however, maintained that the soul is infused at puberty.

Early Christian theologians also disagreed on this matter, with Saint Gregory early in the fourth century maintaining that the soul is infused at conception, while Saint Thomas maintained that this does not occur until the fetus has the form to receive a soul. Other theologians have contended that the embryo is an appendage to the mother until birth. Islam considers life as beginning twelve to eighty days after conception.

Today disagreement on this issue is revealed in many theological conflicts and their interpretations—in hospital rules and procedures, in moral and ethical codes and practices, and in the definitions of morality. So you see the great diversity of judgment on ensoulment.

I would like at this time to call upon Dr. George Corner.

CORNER: For many of us, the topic of our panel—"The Metaphysical Conundrum Concerning the Moment of Ensoulment"—is less than metaphysical; it is meaningless. If the spirit of man, the *anima*, is, as I conceive, an expression—the highest expression—of the physical activities of the living body, then there is no *moment*, of ensoulment, but rather a gradual development of mental and spiritual qualities prepared for *in utero*, which continues from the time of birth and never ceases as long as the body is receptive to environmental stimuli and the mind is capable of memory, attention, reflection, aspiration, and love.

Call this materialism if you will; it is a kind of materialism that finds fullest expression in the language of poetry and religion. It is a philosophy of reverence for life, not for a metaphysical dogma—life that is latent in the human ovum, that develops while in the mother's womb a more and more complex physical organization, is born into the world, grows to maturity and to old age. With it grow the mind and those higher functions of the mind that I call spiritual.

I know that I am speaking as a man of the laboratory to men of practical experience and direct responsibility in the humane professions. I have never been called upon, except in one peculiar case in my own family circle, to share in a decision whether or not to terminate a pregnancy.

For me in that case, as in the many in which you are required to act or to advise, decision would have been easier if I could have regarded the fetus in question as an ensouled person whose eternal career within or without the gates of paradise hung upon the verdict of a little council of doctors, parents, and grandparents in a mundane suburban sitting room.

As I saw it, not one life but two were demanding our reverential consideration: one for which mind and spirit were as yet only potentialities, another for whom they were actualities. I could see no dogmatic solution, yes or no, but a problem calling for balanced judgment and painful decision.

That particular case turned out happily, but members of this panel could, I am sure, cite far more agonizing problems. If they, like this embryologist, see the mind and spirit as functions of the maturing and mature body, they have to make their decisions not by rule but by the far more trying, far more difficult application of human judgment in the individual case.

WASSMER: Now, the point of view of Dr. Joseph Fletcher.

FLETCHER: First of all, this whole question of animation, or the infusion of the soul, seems to me to be nondebatable because it is nonverifiable, nonfalsifiable. The whole issue is over the alleged existence of a metaphysically adumbrated entity or, indeed, entelechy.

As Aristotle might have said, this whole discussion is like the argument about the death of God—pointless because we cannot establish whether God was ever alive to begin with.

All of the positions taken by people about animation are a matter of faith rather than empirical reasoning; therefore, the debate provides no foundation for social policy with respect to abortion.

The second thing I would like to say is that not all Christians, Jews, or Muslims, in the Semitic religions, and, indeed, not all people in the Indic religions, such as Buddhists and Hindus, make any faith affirmation or endorse the soul idea, whether in a creationist, traducian, or eternally pre-existent form.

Third, I want to repeat what I have said before, that our moral criterion should be the desirability of interrupting pregnancies. Our decision should not be determined by questions of viability or inviability, respirated or prerespirated, fertilization or implantation, before or after quickening, or *fetus informatus* or *fetus formatus*.

My plea is that we be situational, not committed to present fabricated rules governing our decisions. Desirability—that is, a bill of goods and evils in any concrete situation realistically assessed in terms of human needs and social welfare—should decide whether we terminate a life *in utero* or postnatally just as we would in any case of self-defense or common defense.

Finally, I want to echo Krister Stendahl's remarks. I think the churches should be lovers of God and have people sensitizing us to human values, not trying to formulate specifications of conduct or rules and moral laws. Therefore, I submit that all soul theory is just another form of the old objective morality and that the attempt to posit a soul is both theologically and ethically unacceptable.

WASSMER: The next speaker is Dr. David Granfield.

GRANFIELD: I am speaking for the life force, the life principle, which makes a human being different from the nonhuman being, which makes the living human different from a thing that is not alive.

However, when we move into it and we try to determine the moment of animation, we also consider whether it is possible to define the embryo or the fetus in such a way that justification for abortion will not also be, at the same time, justification for infanticide and perhaps other types of killing.

The one-celled structure and the multicelled structure have a common cellular denominator in genetic identity. But the baby is not simply an amalgam of genetically identical cells. It has, due to its life principle, a unity as perfect as that of the fertilized ovum. In this context I might bring out a distinction which is often mistaken or overlooked, namely, that when we speak of uniqueness, very often what we are really thinking of or should be thinking of is unity.

Two identical twins share the same unique genetic package, and yet, phenotypically, each one is unique because of the principle of unity that each one shares. They are different people, even though genetically you can see they have the same identical genotype; but phenotypically they are, in terms of actual organism, totally different people.

Let us take a look at some other essential differences. How does the zygote differ from a baby? How does the conceptus differ from the neonate? Fundamentally, it is in the actualizing of the potentialities of the organism by the development of new structures that make new functions possible. This potential is in the zygote; otherwise, it would not be able to realize its particular potentialities, for DNA is found in its full perfection, although not in its full implementation, in man's unicellular beginning. DNA, with the help of RNA, uses twenty different amino acids and develops them into over one hundred thousand proteins which are going to be used to build the body which we will call eventually "a cute little baby." Every bodily part and every bodily process is in some way either a protein or dependent upon a protein.

Now, the very principle of life which initiated the first cell cleavage, after the zygote or fertilized ovum came into being, is the same principle that energizes the complicated intellectual operations facilitated by protein-built structures. Man's most fully human acts are made possible by the multiplicity and differentiation of proteins under the guidance of the vital principle and its informational heritage which is found in the DNA.

From the first, the life force is directed toward protein manufacture, with the ultimate goal of making a suitable instrument for human activity. We call that material instrument of the spirit which builds it a body. The spirit uses body when completed for its specifically human activities just as a scientist who makes a mechanical brain would use that computer for sophisticated intellectual activity, and yet the scientist is not more human because he has that computer. Rather, because he has the computer, he is able to do more human things. The human organism is not more human because it has developed its brain. On the contrary: because it has developed a brain it can do things that are more specifically human.

So, very briefly then, as far as I see it, the life force that sets in motion and directs purposefully the activities of this little one-celled zygote is the same life force that animates the baby and animates every one of us. And if we as adults are human and if the baby is human and animated, so, too, is this initial, though humble, beginning of each one of us.

WASSMER: Our next speaker on the panel is Dr. Andie Knutson.

KNUTSON: My concern is with ethical beliefs and values related to life from conception to burial—and after, if it still is a human life, as some take it to be—with particular reference to what public health and medical people believe in this area. I think we need to recognize that these are the people who will carry out whatever program may be disseminated, and their ethical beliefs and practices are going to be of considerable significance in the way they behave when they deal with these problems.

I offer the interim study of 225 public health professionals. They have been in graduate school for the last several years; they average about 35 years of age; 60 per cent are married; they are highly educated; the median education is 3 years or more in graduate school, some going as high as 7 or 8 years. I have obtained their views, partly by interview and partly by questionnaire. The number of questions unanswered in the questionnaire is less than 10 per cent.

These public health professionals vary as widely in their beliefs as this panel. About half feel that human life begins at conception or during the first trimester; one-sixth during the second or third trimester; and the other third at birth or sometime after birth.

These subjects were queried about the characteristics this new life must have in order for it to be assigned the label "human." The questions I asked were: "When, in the course of this development, would you say this is a human life?" and "What characteristics would you require in order to make that judgment?"

Preliminary study suggests that about 40 per cent believe that it is a new human life when the soul infuses the body. The rest of the subjects offered other criteria for the time when a new life becomes human: when it begins to be perceived, recognized, or felt by the mother; when the father sees it or can feel it; when it is alert and recognizes its environment; when it is physiologically self-sufficient and functioning on its own; when it begins to interact with others and to develop relationships; or when it becomes socialized and has a personality of its own. As you see, these definitions follow an order of progression.

About half in the public health group who are leaders in our society today believe in the God-given or immortal soul. Others believe in a soul of old humanistic definitions, and by that I mean that they believe that the human soul is a useful concept to define awareness, concern, conclusions, attentiveness to others, and ability to distinguish right and wrong. And a smaller but still quite sizable group questioned the validity and usefulness of the concept of soul— as I am sure some of you do. They question the validity and usefulness of this concept and wonder if it doesn't get us into more trouble than not.

It may be of interest that women tend to define a new life as being human earlier than men and by a different set of characteristics than men. They tend to regard it as human when they know it is growing. On the other hand, men do not identify the new life as human until they can see it or communicate with it.

WASSMER: May we hear something about the Jewish tradition from Dr. Israel Margolies.

MARGOLIES: Most of the Jewish scholars from the time of the Talmud down to today, which covers the last two thousand years, were of the opinion that the fetus prior to birth was simply a part of its mother and that this appendage had no individual life, no personality, no personal qualities of its own. It had all the potentiality, the possibilities of spirituality, but could not be called an independent spirit until birth.

This, of course, would mean that we, in considering the question of abortion, need not be concerned about doing away with a human life as long as we are speaking of the prenatal stages. Naturally, we would hopefully expect that, if and when an abortion had to take place, it would be done in the earliest possible stage.

Judaism is essentially a faith that concentrates on this life rather than a future life, and we are often somewhat perplexed at what we consider the overemphasis of some of the other faiths on salvation in terms of life after death. Our major area of concern is this life and what our responsibility is to human strivings, to human goals, and to each other in this life.

It is in this context that we speak of our concern about the human soul. The human soul, which we feel is the one quality that distinguishes us from all other members of the animal kingdom, is discernible in man only from the moment of birth until the moment of death. We leave the problem of what happens after death to those who wish to dabble in that baffling and highly dubious area. If we emphasize life, this life, the world in which we live, and our responsibilities to maintain and enhance life, I think we will be doing more than our share.

WASSMER: Now may we hear from Cyril Means.

MEANS: The question in terms of which this controversy is usually couched is: When does human life begin? This question reminds me of another. A century ago a priest of the Established Church, while strolling down Piccadilly, was accosted by a revivalist preacher, who, with the earnest expression and blade-like look of the true zealot, asked, "Brother, are you saved?" The parson answered, "Yes, I am."

Taken aback by this show of confidence, the Fundamentalist preacher then asked, "When were you saved, brother?"

The padre replied, "More than eighteen hundred years ago, on a barren hill outside Jerusalem."

I believe that the question, When does human life begin? deserves a similar answer. The correct answer is: It does not begin; it began— at least 3.5 million years ago. In other words, all life is one. It is poured into many individual containers, but it is all the same life.

This is an insight which mankind acquired less than a hundred years ago. It was not until 1853 that Ferdinand Keber first observed the union of a spermatozoon with an ovum, but his microscope was incapable of sufficient resolution to reveal the merger of the 23 chromosomes of the spermatozoon with the 23 chromosomes of the ovum into a single group of 46 chromosomes, which constitutes the nucleus of the zygote. The first scientist to observe this phenomenon was Oscar Hertwig, in 1875. In other words, there are a living human spermatozoon and a living human ovum before the moment of fertilization, and all that happens at that moment is that 2 squads of 23 chromosomes each perform a nimble quadrille on the genetic drill-field and rearrange themselves into a platoon of 46. There is no more life, or human life, present after this rearrangement than there was before. Not only is there no more: what life there is is the same as before; it is continuous.

This insight is in marked contrast to the embryological beliefs which prevailed prior to Hertwig's observations. Throughout the Middle Ages, the Aristotelian theory of generation, which assimilated the formation of a fetus from the admixture of semen and catamenia to the curdling of cheese by the admixture of rennet with milk, was the common opinion. Semen and catamenia were, of course, recognized as the products of living human beings, but they were thought of as a sort of refuse which did not share the life of the bodies from which they came.

Francis Wharton, in one of the editions of his treatise on criminal law, cites in a footnote the commentary of an anonymous glossator on one of the provisions of the Corpus Juris Canonici to the following effect. The glossator was explaining the reason why the soul was infused into the male embryo 40 days after conception but into the female embryo 80 days after conception. He refers to the passage in Leviticus which prescribes that a Hebrew mother is ritually unclean for 40 days after she has borne a male child but for 80 days after she has borne a female child, and explains the difference as follows: In the one case, she had carried within herself, at the start of pregnancy, something that was dead for 40 days, while in the other case she had carried the dead thing 80 days.

Why did the glossator think that the fetus was dead for the first 40 or 80 days of pregnancy? Because he considered that the two uncompacted liquids were themselves dead, and that only at the end of this period of time was the fetus formed from them by a curdling process. This strikes our ears as strange only because we no longer believe in abiogenesis. Before the experiments of Lazzaro Spallanzani in the eighteenth century, which Louis Pasteur repeated in the nineteenth, scientists had commonly believed that maggots, for example, were formed from dead and rotting flesh.

It was thus natural for our ancestors to think that there was discontinuity between the lives of the two parents and the life of the offspring. They thought that this hiatus constituted an interval of death between lives. Since Hertwig's observations, we have known that there is no such hiatus, and that there is no interval of death in the seamless web of the continuity of life between that first far-off moment of true abiogenesis on this planet over 3.5 million years ago and the production of each of us as individuals. All life is one, though it is poured into many individual receptacles, just as all wine is one, although it is poured into many wineskins and many bottles.

Let me conclude by making an observation concerning something which Father O'Donnell said at this conference—namely, that the new Codex Juris Canonici, which was promulgated in 1917, requires that an abortive fetus, however young, be baptized. With that much of his statement, I concur. He then went on to say that the baptism which was administered to a very young aborted fetus in accordance with this prescription (Canon 747) of the new Code is baptism *sub conditione*. This is not correct. Canon 747 requires that an abortive fetus, however young, be baptized, not conditionally, but absolutely. This is a radical change from the pre-1917 practice.

Prior to the seventeenth century, it was not the custom to

administer any kind of baptism to an aborted fetus of less than thirty days of fetal age. In the seventeenth century various Roman Catholic physicians and authors began to advocate the conditional baptism of an abortive fetus under thirty days of age, and one of them went so far, in the first edition of his book, as to suggest that anyone who did not conditionally baptize an aborted fetus under thirty days of age was guilty of mortal sin. The Sacred Congregation of the Index in 1666 issued a decree forbidding the further printing of his book until a notice was inserted in the front of it stating that the author did not mean to teach that the failure to administer conditional baptism to so young a fetus constituted mortal sin and that he was discussing the theory of immediate animation only as an academic question. In 1713, the Holy Office issued a further decree which substantially conformed to the 1666 ruling of the Sacred Congregation of the Index.

Nevertheless, these two Roman decisions, while they gave no support to the theory of immediate animation and its practical corollary of conditional baptism of the very young aborted fetus, did not forbid the practice, and that practice, in fact, began to spread, as a matter of pious observance. It was not, however, made compulsory, until the new Code of Canon Law in 1917, and when it was, the form of baptism required to be administered was radically changed from conditional jto absolute. Advocates within the Roman church of the theory of immediate animation have endeavored to make metaphysical mileage out of this new requirement of the 1917 canon. Plausible though their arguments may be, Catholic advocates of the contrary theory of mediate animation point out that it is not by canonical legislation that the church normally solves doctrinal questions.

WASSMER: May we now hear the experience of Dr. Max L. Stackhouse.

STACKHOUSE: The question of animation is the question of when a fetus shall be considered a person and thus when it is subject to the prohibitions against intentional destruction. Anyone clinically, legislatively, or morally facing the problem of abortion in fact answers the animation question operationally. But there is little clarity about what one ought to take into account in arriving at such an operational judgment that allows some fetuses to live and destroys others. Often in the past the question has been answered in terms of "ensoulment" theory, that is, by asking when God makes some sort of supernatural substance intrinsic to the biological fetus. The question is a serious one and must be answered. But since Plato is dead, even if God is not, the whole metaphysical framework by which traditional faith tried to answer this question is highly dubious. Contemporary ethicists speak now of "person" instead of "soul."

I should like to suggest that in order to be a person, an existent must be (1) in the genetic continuity of *Homo sapiens*, (2) in an organic or economic relationship that demands allocation of energy resources in the direction of the existent, (3) capable of interactive relationships with another, and (4) in a community context that can and does recognize the significance of the reality of the existent.

1. To be in genetic relationship with the species *Homo sapiens* suggests that the minimal biological and genetic characteristics must be present that would allow the other relations to develop. If that genetic base is not present, no personhood exists, and destruction is permissible whether the genetic base is distorted from conception, disease, accidental use of medication, or some other cause. The probability of non-*Homo sapiens* is presumed to be an empirically determinable question and should be dealt with by medically trained personnel acting in accord with the best standards of science available. If a fetus, genetically defective to the point where it may never engage in conscious attempts to sustain relational existence, is not destroyed and proceeds through the other relationships, he may be removed from the genetic stream by humane institutional isolation.

2. To be in an organic or economical relationship suggests that minimal conditions of systemic interchange of energy take place between the existent and surrounding resources. If that relationship is not established, as in "tubal pregnancies" and prior to implantation, no personhood exists and destruction is permissible. Thus, for example, those forms of birth control that prevent implantation after fertilization are not subject to any restrictive principles that may

derive from moral reflection on abortion. Further, when implantation has occurred, but the continued existence of the fetus would demand reallocation of limited biochemical resources so as to endanger the health of the mother or the reallocation of economic resources of the community so as to endanger other developed persons, the pregnancy may be interrupted. More fully developed relationships are morally preferable to subpersonal existents.

When a genetic relationship and an organic relationship are established, a *potential* person can be said to exist, although it is not an *actual* person until the other relationships are established. "Animation," the minimal addition of "super-natural" qualities, has not necessarily occurred. Nevertheless it is possible that under certain conditions it could occur. Hence related life, even in this minimal sense, is valuable and should be protected from wanton destruction even if it does not and should not come under the legal or moral protections granted persons.

3. The implicit requirement of actual personhood that calls for interactive relationships to others suggests the necessity of a sustained sociopsychological context sufficiently defined to allow at least rudimentary redefinition of the identity of those involved in the relationship. That phenomenon begins as soon as there is consciousness on the part of at least the mother that the relationship will require a change in her identity. The traditional doctrine of mediate animation can be seen as an attempt to deal with this human phenomenon of a change in the status of the fetus taking place when the mother feels movement. With the development of the medical technology that can confirm presence and relationship at an earlier stage, the criterion is pushed closer to the times of genetic and organic relations. If, however, the identity of the mother is discernibly not open to redefinition, that is, for example, if she cannot get married (and, very significantly, change her name) in a situation where marriage is required for childbearing, or cannot psychically stand the change to "mother" without serious closing and destruction of the capacity to interact in established relationships, the parties may be separated. It is morally preferable if the potential person is preserved from destruction and relocated in a situation where interactive relationships can occur.

The capacity to separate and relocate, however, depends in later stages of pregnancy on the adoptive or institutional arrangements of a society and, in earlier stages, the level of medical technology and resources available to preserve the fetus. Where these are not available and the destruction of identity-forming relations seems inevitable, separation may be necessary before community relationships are developed, even if it means the death of the fetus.

4. Three kinds of phenomena are relevant in the relationship of the fetus to the community—legal, religiocultural, and sociocultural— each of which claims formal or informal sanctity. First, it is notable that most medical law does not require that an aborted fetus prior to twenty weeks have a birth, death, or stillborn certificate, although some recent legislation has specified sixteen weeks.

In any case, after a specified time such a record is required. Thus there is a legal-political time for an institutionally validated, formal recognition of actual existence of a "person" of sufficient status to have a permanent place in the official memory of society.

Closely related is the growing practice of awarding damages to an unborn child who, because of injury to the mother, is born prematurely and dies. There are many and various cases on this, but, to my knowledge, one of the most striking of these cases ethically is an April 1967 decision by the Massachusetts Supreme Court, which awarded such damages to a fetus harmed at three and a half months that died soon after birth two months later. It is not clear whether damages would have been awarded if the fetus had aborted and died immediately in the accident.

What is interesting, however, is the court's suggestion, in reversing a Justice Holmes decision of 1884, that such matters vary in different settings. This suggestion is compatible with a relational definition of personhood that sees different kinds of societies producing and defining personhood differently, a phenomenon that would require a sliding scale of protection according to the situation. The court's decision *implies* that under changing conditions of available medical technology and extended protection of individual rights, the tendency is to slide the scale of legally recognized personhood toward earlier stages of fetal growth.

There also seems to be a religiocultural recognition of a qualitative distinction between later and earlier fetal development in the absence of baptism and funeral rites for an early aborted fetus, even if some residues of life exist. Nor, to my knowledge, have the churches or synagogues ever allocated burial space for such a fetus. A fetus aborted after four and a half to five months is offered such rites and space by the religious institutions, indicating a functional recognition of qualitative difference.

The implications of the attempt to redefine personhood in ethical and relational rather than intrinsic or metaphysically infused terms can be grouped in three sets: ethical, theological, and social.

Ethically, this view better accounts for the reasons, moral and legal, already given to grant exemptions to widespread prohibitions against abortion than do usual reasons. Relational reasons are closer to the normative definition of the ethos. Allowing abortion for reasons of rape and incest, for example, involves a judgment about the relationships that are decisive for the definition of the person-hood of the fetus, not about the genetic condition or "soul" of that fetus.

Allowing abortion because of probability of danger to the health of the mother is, in fact, a judgment based on the nature of a relationship rather than on the intrinsic properties or spiritual status of a fetus. When psychiatric and socioeconomic indicators are introduced, as they are in many deliberations of conscientious women desiring abortion, relational considerations are given priority over intrinsic ones, often with disastrous consequences because of the need to find illegal means to carry out moral decisions. Further, the clear indications that there are direct correlations between urbaniza-tion rates and abortion rates reinforces the claim that the nature of the community relationship is a functionally normative considera-tion in the definition of personhood.

Theologically, the relational view speaks to the same ultimate questions that a more traditional, metaphysical one does, but it offers some answers that pertain more directly to the empirical conditions of mankind. It points to facets of human personality that are "supernatural" and that are fundamental to the foundations of responsible behavior.

Such a view claims to determine what sensitivities should be in the minds of clinicians and potential mothers and in the laws of society. For it directs our attention to the clarification and criticism of hidden presuppositions that govern policy, decision, and legal order by asking what ought to be considered of ultimate worth and power in human affairs. And such considerations are what, functionally, theologians mean by the word "God."

In this view, whenever there are not only the genetic and organic relationships, but also interactive and community relationships, actual personhood exists and "ensoulment," if one must use the term, can be said to have occurred. Theologically, it can be said that the divine-human relationship is established.

There seems no alternative but to remove abortion from the range of punishable crimes and the proscriptions of medical policy. In fact, it is highly likely that this would entail the keeping of medical records on abortions, a kind of community-sanctioned memory of the existence of at least a potential person. Thus abolition of abortion laws would tend functionally and legally to give more status to the fetus than present procedures, which often force medical personnel to deal with the fetus through an ordinary dilatation and curettage operation and illegal abortionists wantonly to destroy potential persons.

However, repeal of abortion laws is not a full solution; it is only the removal of a structural impediment to the finding of some solutions. A fuller picture of the social implications of a relational theological ethic would also include a massive assault on those conditions that presently make abortion necessary. Such an assault would surely include making contraceptives and "morning after" medication safe, effective, and available and ministering to the poverty communities at home and abroad to increase their energy and economic resources. That is the first responsibility of those concerned about the preservation of human life.

It is also necessary to develop counseling clinics to help persons, couples, or families sort out and strengthen relationships that would snap under additional pressure and to broaden their conception of the alternatives of immediate abortion or childbearing. A well-designed counseling clinic or pastoral care center is necessary for long-range effectiveness in value orientation. In addition, medical and legal personnel should be further sensitized to the ways in which kinds and qualities of relationships in the context of society are decisive for definitions of health, life, and personhood. And, finally, as these become focuses of attention, the community at large may be called upon to allocate funds for medical research that attempts to preserve relational existence in the later stages of pregnancy, and for the legal protection of persons step by step into earlier months of pregnancy according to the level of medical technology and the capacity of the mother and the community to interact with and acknowledge genuine relationships.

ABORTION AND POVERTY

The Social Discrimination Involved in the Practice of Abortion

Joseph D. Beasley, M.D. (moderator)
Philip M. Sarrel, M.D. (rapporteur)
Lawrence Lader
Kenneth R. Niswander, M.D.
Percy E. Sutton, LL.B.
Kenneth R. Whittemore

BEASLEY: I realize that this is an international conference on abortion, yet many of the things said here may not relate to other countries. In this panel discussion we will speak of the social discrimination involved in the practice of abortion in the United States. Various other panel members will elaborate further on specific aspects of this problem, but I would like first to place the problem in the context of our health care systems as I perceive them.

Out of a population of over 200 million people, about 150 million receive their medical services from some form of private practice paid for either by themselves or by third-party sources. The other 50 million receive their care from some sort of tax-supported service or receive no care at all. In general the health care received by this segment of the population can be characterized as episodic, disease-oriented, intermittent, or not available. The balance of my comments will be concerned with contrasting the social discrimination involved in the practice of abortion among this estimated one-fourth of the population as compared to the other three-fourths.

We do not know the exact number of "criminal abortions" that occur in the United States, but there is considerable evidence that so-called therapeutic abortions performed by professionals in hospitals occur with a much higher frequency among the more affluent than they do among the poor. There is also considerable evidence to indicate that complications resulting from criminal abortion occur at a higher frequency among the poor than among the middle and upper classes. This has led some to believe that the rate of abortion among the lower socioeconomic group is higher than among the middle and upper socioeconomic groups; however, my evaluation of the data that are available and my own experience would indicate that this is not the case. How do we account, then, for the lower incidence of therapeutic abortion available to the poor in the United States, on the one hand, and the seemingly higher incidence of severe complications observed as a result of abortion among this population, on the other?

In my opinion, the differences observed in these two populations can best be explained by certain characteristics that we have observed and measured among the poverty group that are different from those among the middle and upper socioeconomic groups. Our studies in the metropolitan area of New Orleans and probability samples of the population of the United States have demonstrated a marked discrepancy between the knowledge of family planning and the most elementary aspects of reproductive physiology among the poor as compared to the more affluent of our society. Of course many people in the middle and upper socioeconomic groups understand very little about reproductive physiology, but the great majority of them practice contraception. This is not the case, however, among those in the poverty group. They not only do not understand the elementary aspects of reproductive physiology, but they also lack access to the information and services that would allow them to prevent unwanted pregnancies.

The incidence of unwanted pregnancies occurring both in the unmarried woman under nineteen and in the older married woman with several children has been found to be much higher among the lower socioeconomic group than among the middle and upper socioeconomic groups. It has been shown repeatedly that when adequate services are made available in a humane fashion to the poor they will rapidly utilize them and decrease the number of unwanted pregnancies.

The discrimination against the poor in regard to both education and the availability of adequate contraceptive services is in my opinion the major cause of the high rate of unwanted pregnancies observed in this population.

Once an unwanted pregnancy occurs in the poor patient, she is at a considerable disadvantage. Most of these women lack the sophistication to consider the possibility of a therapeutic abortion and the aggressiveness to pursue this through the institutions of medical care that are available to them. Those women who do attempt to arrange an induced abortion in tax-supported institutions are almost always denied a hearing of their case. Therefore, once the avenue of therapeutic abortion performed in a hospital setting under legal circumstances has been denied to the small minority of poor patients who have the sophistication to seek such an abortion, the alternative is to have an unwanted child or to seek an abortion in the open market. Unfortunately, safe abortions performed outside of the law are quite expensive and require referral contacts from the private sector of the medical profession. Since the poor patient has neither access to the private sector nor the ability to raise the funds necessary, she may either submit to a cheap, crudely performed, and hence dangerous abortion or bear an unwanted child. Fear is another factor that tends to reduce the number of abortions among the poor. Many have observed the serious medical complications suffered by friends and relatives from crude abortions performed outside the law.

In my opinion, marked social discrimination against the poor in the practice of abortion exists in the United States. This problem is part of a more complex one that involves the whole health care system available to the poor in the United States: a lack of adequate family-planning information and services for the entire population, but particularly the unavailability of this type of information to the lower socioeconomic group, and the exclusion of the indigent in abortion cases from the tax-supported institutions on a medicolegal basis and from the private sector of medicine on a financial basis. Hence the problem of social discrimination against the poor in the practice of abortion is inextricably related to the broader problem of discrimination against that segment of the United States population who reside in poverty.

The various members of the panel will now elaborate further on particular aspects of this problem. I will first ask Mr. Whittemore to comment upon the availability of criminal abortions in a metropolitan area.

WHITTEMORE: The most desirable resource for a "nonlegal" abortion is an obstetrician who would be willing to perform such an operation in a local hospital. Discussion with several physicians indicates that such decisions are made on occasion if there is minimum risk of legal involvement. These considerations generally mean that the physician is more apt to perform such a procedure on one of his regular patients. This selective process works to the disadvantage of the lower-income female since she often depends on clinic services and does not have a private obstetrician. In the general hospital that I studied, less than 5 per cent of the lab results that revealed "evidence of fetus" from D's and C's where the patient was not listed as pregnant were from service patients, although they accounted for close to 50 per cent of the patient population. Conversations with interns and residents on the obstetrical and gynecological ward produced ready testimony that such involvement with clinic patients was avoided.

One abortionist who operated in a clearly criminal manner and who accounted for the largest number of such abortions in the community by far, asked for a standard fee of $150, obviously out of the reach of the poor. Still, he often performed his services for less money and on rare occasion charged nothing. His reasons were twofold: (1) having decided to do what was asked, he did not want to increase his risks by having to have persons return with more money at a later date; and (2) he further referred to himself as a "poor country boy" who never intended to get rich, but who only wanted to "help out"—thus money was not seen as his only concern. Such procedures did not work as much to the benefit of the poor in the community as might be imagined, however, since his peculiar judgmental attitudes often screened them out for other than economic reasons. His acceptance of reduced fees generally involved college students who could not get the full amount without arousing suspicions and was not because of an inability to gain funds per se.

The discussion of abortion and the poor is complicated by the presence of a self-fulfilling-prophecy effect that has been operating for decades. Originally, it might be conjectured, more purely economic considerations gave the poor less access to abortion. The result was that more females in the lower classes bore children out of wedlock. This led to such behavior being subjected to a lessening degree of negative sanction, which may now result in those in similar socioeconomic circumstances having fewer pressures placed upon them to seek out an abortionist.

The problem is further complicated by the fact that income and functional intelligence are often related, the lower-class, less well educated person often not knowing as much about available alternatives and resources as her economically wealthier counterpart.

Again, race is a complicating factor. For example, one of the abortionists in the community was a Negro practical nurse and midwife. Her regular fee was such that most of her clients were white. Further, those abortions she did perform on nonwhites were done for either (1) those who could pay the fee asked, or (2) those who had some direct or indirect means of personal contact with her, for whom she provided services at a reduced fee—but never free. What often appears to be a racial factor, in other words, may be primarily an economic one.

It would surprise no one that the differential disadvantage to which the poor are subjected was manifested in two dramatic ways: (1) A higher rate of medical complications resulted from attempts at self-induced abortion, especially among poor nonwhites. (2) The poorest-trained and most dangerous of the available criminal abortionists served primarily the poor. For example, the garage mechanic whose friend, expelled from medical school, had taught him how to insert a catheter into the cervix, performed abortions primarily on the younger, nonwhite girls who partially met his demand for payment by allowing him to have sex with them beforehand, then paying whatever they could (usually between $15 and $35). Because of a combination of factors—their young age, their race, their inability to pay a reasonable fee—these girls would normally be refused as clients by the better qualified abortionists in the community.

BEASLEY: Mr. Lader will now give us some information about abortion-referral services.

LADER: I know of four referral services for extrahospital abortion in the United States. First, the Society for Humane Abortion in San Francisco, which distributes an information sheet mainly listing

Mexican doctors. While I have never seen these clinics firsthand, my understanding from California doctors who have checked the results is that, while some Mexican doctors are reasonably good, many are poor. Cases demanding a skilled surgeon are frequently referred to me in New York.

The second source is the Parents' Aid Society on Long Island, New York, which handles a few dozen referrals a week. They use a long list of Eastern doctors who are not rigidly screened.

The third source is the Clergyman's Consultation Service of New York, made up of about twenty-five ministers and rabbis who handle consultations on a rotating basis—at least 2,000 in the last two years. Calls come to a number listed in the telephone directory. The women are given the names of clergymen on duty that day. In their interviews with applicants, the clergymen discuss various alternatives such as hospital abortion, bearing the child, solving marital problems, and adoption.

If abortion appears the only solution (as happens in 90 per cent of the cases), most referrals are made to Puerto Rico, where prices now run about $500 plus air fare and hotel. Medical standards there vary greatly. Recent referrals have been made to London where surgery, plane, and hotel can run almost $1,000. A few ministers, however, used skilled surgeons from my Eastern group whom I consider comparable to London at far lower cost. The question of whether all ministers should use these local surgeons is now being debated.

Clerical services in other cities are being formed, but only those in Los Angeles and New Jersey are operating, with Philadelphia's in the process of formation. A sizable grant of money has recently been given to further the growth of this movement.

The fourth source is my personal referral service, which has handled almost 600 cases in the last 2 years. From lengthy letters by applicants, and a 50-part questionnaire answered by almost 300 women, we now have the first sizable study of attitudes and results in skilled, extrahospital abortion.

My aim has been to keep the highest medical standards at the lowest prices. All participants are obstetrician-gynecologists. Three of the four are diplomates of the Board of Obstetrics and Gynecology. One operates in the South, the others in New York or nearby cities.

The fee is $300 or $400. Surgery is performed in the doctor's office—
10 weeks of pregnancy or less preferred, with cases rarely taken at
11 or 12 weeks. A nurse is in attendance and local anesthesia used.
Patients from distant states may be allowed to sleep in the doctor's
office overnight, and an associate often provides personal services
like meeting a woman who is traveling alone at the airfield. All
doctors have regular practices and give about 10 or 20 per cent of
their time to abortion.

How available are these services? As far as I can judge, they are
completely available to anyone with the intelligence to find them.
The San Francisco service, Parents' Aid, and Clergymen's Consultation have all been highly publicized, and a patient need only consult
newspaper files. In my own case, the patient checking a library could
find my book, numerous articles I have written, or articles about my
work in newspapers and other periodicals.

Significantly, an increasing number of physicians in New York
have sent me their patients. Doctors at a few universities keep
magazine articles of mine on their desk and hand them to prospective patients. A few staff members at Planned Parenthood chapters
make referrals to me—which should increase now that the Planned
Parenthood Federation has accepted abortion as part of total birth
control.

Unfortunately, the basic attitude of the medical profession
remains a timorous one. A minority of doctors help their patients,
generally with vague clues. Those who help almost never refer
directly, but send patients to a service.

The greatest problem is that I have not been able to find a skilled
surgeon in the Middle or Far West who will accept referrals.
Therefore, patients must come from as far as California and British
Columbia to the East and South.

But beyond these services with skilled surgeons, what is available?
While many doctors and unqualified personnel perform abortions
around the country, none to my knowledge meet rigid standards. A
former doctor who performed abortions widely years ago, for
example, has returned to abortion, but in my view is no longer up to
required standards.

What is available to the poor? Few people in poverty brackets are
getting to referral services. I have handled a fair number of patients

with incomes under $5,000 and a small percentage of Negroes and Puerto Ricans. But despite the fact that surgeons have taken some women at $200 and even $100, the unfortunate conclusion is that we are not really reaching the poverty cases.

Yet we know that far too many people are going to local midwives and hacks. Harlem Hospital receives about 400 botched abortions a year; another on the fringe of Harlem gets 250 to 300. Many never appear in abortion statistics, since staffs are humane enough to keep them from police reports if possible.

Should not the reform movement be making an effort to reach poverty cases? Since they rarely read the *New York Times* or similar media, should the services not go directly to Harlem and other poverty areas with ads in the *Amsterdam News* or *Ebony*?

Finally, what are the medical consequences from good referral services? I cannot speak for Puerto Rican or Mexican clinics, of which I have grave doubts. But all surgeons I use follow up each case by phone a day later, and again a week or two later. In almost 600 cases, not one incident of damage has been reported. Patient reaction both physically and psychologically has been overwhelmingly favorable. Reports of pain during surgery have been minimal. Most women state they would return to skilled abortion again if necessary.

If I may be permitted a personal conclusion, I would like to urge the reform movement to support all good referral services, both clerical and lay. They seem to me the most direct and effective attack on the present cruel and hypocritical system.

BEASLEY: Dr. Niswander, would you talk about the intrahospital or therapeutic abortion and whether it is available to the poor.

NISWANDER: Discrimination against the poor in the availability of legal hospital abortion is easy to document. Dr. Robert Hall surveyed 60 major hospitals throughout the United States and found the incidence of therapeutic abortion to be enormously higher among private patients than among ward patients. To state the extremes, one hospital reported a therapeutic abortion rate of 1 per 37 deliveries among its private patients while another hospital reported no abortions among 24,013 indigent patients delivered. Dr. Edwin

Gold et al. reported a tenfold higher incidence among private patients than among clinic patients in New York City. Although many others report similar discrimination against the poor, there is some evidence that this double standard of care may be giving way. Although our experience in Buffalo has generally paralleled that reported by Dr. Hall, we have noted some change during the past two or three years.

We have performed increasing numbers of abortions on clinic patients and also on private Negro patients, frequently with no professional charge. It is to be hoped that a similar trend may be reported from other centers and that the trend will grow. There is in Buffalo an active effort underway at least to listen to the clinic patient who asks for an abortion.

As a first step toward its cure, the etiology of this discrimination should be determined; why does it exist? We can supply a partial list of answers. The pregnant woman whose economic and cultural background is similar to her doctor's can better explain her emotional state to him; he, in turn, can empathize with her. The poor patient may not trust the doctor enough to talk about her emotional problems or she may not be able to explain her feelings to him. In many cases, she may not even try. She may get lost, as Dr. Beasley has pointed out, in the maze of the medical system.

Delay in obtaining necessary appointments with medical consultants or inability to secure her husband's consent for abortion may pose such serious obstacles for the clinic patient that she may give up the effort; or the long wait to see the busy professional man may drive her to the illegal abortionist. A hospital abortion may be more expensive than a criminal abortion, and she may find hospital care simply not worth the extra money, especially with the greater effort needed to secure approval for the abortion.

Or the indigent patient may overhear conversations among the medical staff ridiculing her for the unwanted pregnancy and her desire to terminate it. If she is a Negro, she may overhear the doctor suggesting that the Negro culture readily accepts the out-of-wedlock child and that there is, therefore, no need for pregnancy interruption in the young unmarried Negro woman. She feels ashamed of being pregnant, though unmarried, no matter what the doctors say, but how can she tell her doctor about it?

Many other reasons for the obvious discrimination against the poor in making therapeutic abortions available could be cited. Clearly, we do not treat the poor patient in the same way we care for the more affluent. Nor do we feel as comfortable with a patient in an unstable social situation as with one in a stable marital relationship. Few clinic doctors, for example, would even talk about abortion to a pregnant widow who is the sole financial and emotional support of her two teen-age children. Who, may I ask, needs an abortion more desperately than such a woman?

If we could learn to listen, really listen, to our clinic patients, perhaps we might have fewer septic abortions filling our wards. Hospital abortions obviously must be made more available to all who need them, including the indigent. It would appear that a trend is beginning in this direction, but it is not nearly strong enough to date.

BEASLEY: Dr. Sarrel will now tell us about his experience with the abortion problem in unmarried teen-agers.

SARREL: I would like to state that my experience has been as an obstetrician caring for teen-age pregnant girls in the poverty group in New Haven. Ninety-eight per cent of the patients have been Negro. In this group certain characteristics must be appreciated in order to understand the place of abortion as a solution to problem pregnancies.

First of all, criminal abortion is a rare occurrence among unmarried poor minors. They cannot afford to pay an abortionist, they have little access to one, and abortionists avoid becoming involved with such youngsters. In a series of 100 teen-age maternity patients cared for at Yale, a 5-year follow-up was done. During the follow-up period the group conceived an additional 249 pregnancies. Only 9 ended in abortion and only 5 of those were septic abortions.

The low number of abortions documented in the group cited indicates the lack of availability of this service for the group. It should also be noted that no therapeutic abortions were done for any of the group despite the fact that many of the girls were quite young, the oldest being 17 at the time of her initial pregnancy. One 13-year-old claimed that her pregnancy was the result of rape. She was not qualified for abortion, but was able to have her baby adopted.

It is important to realize that pregnancy for an unwed Negro teen-ager is often a most meaningful event and that abortion is the solution that is least desired. That is, within the culture of poverty there can exist a set of circumstances, of psychosocial factors, that determine a need to become pregnant despite the fact that a girl is not married. For example, a boyfriend's prestige may depend upon his ability to impregnate his girlfriend, or all of a girl's peer group may have become pregnant. Under these circumstances pregnancies occur because there is a need to become pregnant that is greater than the need not to become pregnant. Failure to appreciate such needs and jumping to abortion as the solution to teen-age out-of-wedlock pregnancy is a mistake, for abortion will only solve the immediate crisis and if not combined with ongoing care will prove to be merely a temporary measure in a long reproductive lifetime.

Our approach, in New Haven, has been to provide the multipro-fessional services that teen-age girls require during their pregnan-cies. Through education, peer-group interaction, and continuity of medical, social, and educational services, we have aimed at channel-ing needs that resulted in pregnancy into other areas of develop-ment. As a result, we have experienced a low rate of repeat pregnancy and a high rate of continued education. Among those girls who have had repeat pregnancies—less than 10 per cent of the total group—a number of pregnancies have been a result of contra-ceptive failure. In-hospital abortion has been made available to this group, but has been accepted by only three of the girls. During the last three years there has been one illegal abortion in the entire group (approximately 200 girls). Our impression is that abortion will be meaningful to the poor when the desperate need to be pregnant is replaced by other outlets for self-expression. Certainly, for this group, which represents such a high risk in their pregnancies, the minimum that the physician can do is to make contraception as well as legal abortion available.

BEASLEY: Our last panelist is Mr. Sutton, who will speak about abortion in the Negro ghetto.

SUTTON: My sponsorship of the abortion reform law in New York grew out of some of the experiences I had in practicing law in the ghetto. At a time when many of the countries in this world are at the peak of their production, there is still a culture of poverty.

When we talk about poverty we often talk of the immorality, the promiscuity, and the "curious habits" of the poor. But how immoral are the poor? Are abortions among the poor immoral? Are the poor more promiscuous than the rich? The poor work at our hospitals and observe the legal abortions permitted the rich. The poor work in the homes of the rich and they know when the daughter is sent away to a different state or country for an abortion—the poor are often *too* well informed and so they really know something about the immorality of the rich.

I have some statistics that show the discrimination against the poor in the practice of abortion in New York City hospitals. In the municipal hospitals, with 18,000 ward beds, there were only 109 legal abortions within a recent one-year period. During the same period, in private hospitals, with only 4,500 beds, 1,731 abortions were performed.

I would also like to tell you about a survey I did in 1966 in connection with some articles on abortion that I was writing for a New York newspaper. This survey revealed part of the abortion picture in the poor communities of the southwest Bronx, Harlem, and Bedford-Stuyvesant. I talked to 105 people, all of whom had committed abortions during the first 6 months of 1966. Among these people there were 8 doctors, 8 medical school dropouts, 12 nurses, 18 nurses' aides, 14 other hospital employees, 3 ambulance drivers, 18 beauticians, a barber, a stenotype operator, a schoolteacher, a bus driver, 5 automobile mechanics, a veterinarian, a chiropractor, a marriage counselor, 2 automobile mechanics, 2 liquor-store employees, and 8 employees at homes for unwed mothers.

One of the nurses did quite a large business. She had, in the period under study, done 187 abortions. Her average fee was $400. She was a black woman from my own Harlem community. She seldom did abortions on black people, however; she specialized in unmarried schoolteachers. She was discriminatory and would not accept a married woman. With three assistants, she operated off a small boat that was located sometimes near La Guardia Airport, sometimes on the Hudson River, and sometimes at a yacht basin in Westchester. Most of her clients were white; the poor blacks in her own neighborhood could not afford her fee.

Two of the doctors, both black, had gotten into trouble. It is worth noting what happens to doctors from poor communities who get into trouble as abortionists, so let me give you their case histories in brief. One of them sometimes took payment for his abortions "in trade." He said that at least one out of every three abortions he performed was done in return for an act of sexual intercourse with the patient.

The one was a Howard University Medical School graduate, and the other had attended New York University Medical School. The doctor from Howard was addicted to drugs; he did abortions for the purpose of continuing his addiction. He charged $150 and reported that he did not have a single failure in the 700 or so abortions he did. He also had a working relationship with a Harlem hospital in case he failed on a patient.

Incidentally, one of the problems in the black community is that doctors, who might do otherwise if they were at Mount Sinai Hospital in New York where they would have access to a medical board that would give legal approval to a warranted abortion, are driven to referring their patients to illegal abortionists. You might ask whether this practice is not a simple matter of economics. The answer is that it is partly a matter of money and partly a matter of color. There are social contacts between even the wealthy black father, who discovers his daughter is pregnant, and the doctor who can give her a legal abortion. But how does the poor black father approach it? He does not play golf with the doctor at Mount Sinai who could find that his daughter comes within the scope of those who might legally have an abortion. So what does he do? He contacts the drug addict from Howard University, the illegal abortionist.

Now let us look at what happened to these two black abortionists after they were caught. In the first place, how were they discovered? You know the story. A young lady ends up with a poor job done on her and she stumbles into a hospital. There is a policeman on duty at the hospital in the poorer areas. Because of the policeman's presence, the doctor on duty finds it wise and expedient to report the suspected act of abortion to the policeman. The policeman interviews the patient and immediately takes her into custody. She is asked about the abortion. She is booked as an accessory, but because she does not have money she does not get a lawyer, and if her bail is set high she cannot get bail money. When the Legal Aid or assigned lawyer talks to her he tells her that she can plead to a health law violation and avoid further trouble as an accessory. More than likely she will agree to plead guilty to a health law. Now, as a condition to being allowed to plead guilty to a health law violation she promises to turn in the person who committed the abortion.

Because some states have rather strong evidential procedures regarding the law, we usually find the requirement that someone else be a witness to the abortion. This usually means bringing in the husband or the boyfriend, who will try to save his own hide by testifying against the doctor or other party who committed the abortion. Thus it is that out of the poverty of the patient will come the conviction of the abortionist.

Now, if my discussion seems in the nature of an indictment, it is not so intended. What I do intend to focus upon is the large job that needs to be done in poor areas in the matter of abortions and their social consequences.

Of the 90 persons who have recently gone to trial in New York State for abortions in Bronx County, Queens County, New York County, and Nassau County, 69 were convicted.

But let me go back to my doctors. Both of them are again practicing medicine—the "addict" and the "lecher." But they are practicing because they had made enough money as abortionists to employ competent legal services. Both worked rather diligently throughout the court procedures performing more abortions so as to be able to pay to have lawyers defend them. This leads to the realization that when we discuss the laws in the United States and foreign countries that prohibit freedom of abortion, we should consider the bad social consequences to all who touch the aborted women—the husband or the boyfriend, the doctor or other person who does the abortion, and the lawyer who finally represents the abortionist.

We should also consider the effect of these laws upon the lives of poor people who do not have access to the better hospitals and have access only to the back-room abortionists. The courts and the police deal severely with these people. In having an illegal abortion, poor women, then, expose themselves to great legal as well as medical risks.

BEASLEY: I would like to open up the discussion to the other experts, and I wonder if anyone would like to challenge anything said so far.

LADER: Mr. Sutton, if a woman does not give the information the police want, is she ever put in jail?

SUTTON: Oh, yes.

HARDIN: If a lawyer handles her case, can't she get out?

SUTTON: Yes, but too often not immediately. She is likely to be held overnight as an accessory, and bail is likely to be set beyond her ability to pay. And the fact I wish to impress upon you is that the period of her confinement and the amount of her bail induce her to testify against the abortionist.

HARDIN: Why doesn't the Legal Aid Society give the proper legal aid?

SUTTON: My own experience is that too often a Legal Aid Society lawyer in the Criminal Court is obliged to represent so many people in one day that he is unable to give truly effective representation to any. He is assigned so many clients that he cannot even effectively *interview* all of them. Witness this: the presiding judge in a crowded Criminal Court has a Legal Aid Society lawyer before him. Let us say the Legal Aid lawyer is representing twenty people. The judge may bargain with him by saying, "Suppose we let this one go; let's prosecute this one, and I'll be easy on the next." This is, I am afraid, what occasionally happens.

LADER: I know two hospitals where the doctors do not report abortions unless they are really septic. They seem to make an honest attempt not to involve the woman.

SUTTON: There is a good deal of that attitude in the wealthier neighborhoods, but unfortunately in the poor neighborhoods there is pressure on the doctor. By the time he sees the patient other persons have also seen her, and he isn't going to jeopardize his position by protecting the patient and covering up an illegal abortion.

SARREL: At Yale the diagnosis on admission of these patients is incomplete abortion, not septic abortion, and the police would never interview a patient whose diagnosis is incomplete abortion, so we never see the policeman anymore.

P. DIGGORY: We have a different system in England. It would be very dangerous for any one of our doctors to give a diagnosis to a policeman. It is quite impossible for a doctor to give an opinion without the patient's permission. Either the doctor or the nurse would be struck off the official register if a patient complained about this happening. Such matters are treated as a direct confidence between the physician and his patient, and this confidence is respected in both the legal and the medical worlds. Why, if a patient complained that I told even her husband that she had had a criminal abortion, I would be hauled before the General Medical Committee.

TYLER: In Cleveland, Ohio, our situation is much closer to Mr. Diggory's, in that there is no breech of confidence unless the patient is brought to the emergency room by the police and they require information of a specific nature from the examining physician.

D. HALL: I am from the Los Angeles County Health Department. My work involves, in part, dealing with the problems of poor people in Mexican and Negro communities. We now have one year's experience with a new, so-called liberalized abortion law, and the results are quite interesting. I have heard a lot of people say that this is step Number One, but for the poor it is not; it is step Number One only for the affluent people in our community, and as far as the poor are concerned it may be a step backward.

In Los Angeles, we have three county hospitals and are very fortunate that the largest of these hospitals happens to have a Director of Obstetrics who is interested in the problem of abortion.

The other two county general hospitals will not touch it, although all three are under the same County administration. If you send a patient who qualifies completely to be sterilized, for example, an even less controversial procedure, at the very last minute a resident can himself make the decision that this woman is not going to get the operation. He can make this decision for reasons of his own without considering the woman's problems. There is no recourse.

There is a great need to inform women of their rights. I have not found anyone in our department who routinely tells women about the availability of legal abortion even if they qualify under the restrictions of the new law. They do not, for example, tell young girls the first time they see them, "If you are fourteen and pregnant you will automatically be eligible for abortion if you want it."

I think it is one thing to say poor people are ignorant of the law, but I think it is the responsibility of officials to make sure that they know about the law so that people are able to make a choice which is based upon their own beliefs.

SARREL: The most effective abortion program I have seen is in Yugoslavia, where the poor can have an abortion at will; but this can be overdone. One of the patients I saw, for example, was about to have her fifth abortion in two years, when she suddenly changed her mind, got up from the operating table, and decided to go through with the pregnancy. This story illustrates one of my concerns about the practice of abortion, namely, that it tends to become depersonalized and to place too little value on the deep-seated human problems involved. I am concerned with people leading better lives, and if you have abortion committees operating in a vacuum you don't improve people's lives at all. In New Haven, as another example, 20 per cent of our abortion patients came back pregnant, because we did not provide adequate follow-up care.

HARDIN: This sort of argument always disturbs me. It is like the people who run down birth control by saying that we should be producing more food. We need both; but, of the two, which is easier, practicing contraception or solving the problem of more food? The problem of contraception is miniscule compared to the other one and it seems to me that the issue here is that it is much easier to perform abortions than to remake the lives of all the women who want them. Granted, the remaking of many of these lives would be admirable, but it is hardly practical.

SARREL: I don't think that we should substitute doing abortions for responding to the needs of human life.

HARDIN: There is not enough time to follow your suggestion now. Today we must do the abortions. Tomorrow we can work on the more basic problems.

SUTTON: We were discussing poverty and how much a change in the practice of abortions would affect the poor. Dr. Sarrel, may I say that the social problem remains. We have made some general progress; but none of the minor reforms in the abortion laws will, in my belief, have any effect on the poor. The poor will not be benefited until these laws are completely repealed.

ABORTION AND PUBLIC HEALTH

The Medical Ravages Consequent to Extrahospital Abortions

Milton Helpern, M.D. (moderator)
Edwin M. Gold, M.D. (rapporteur)
Roberto Bachi, Ph.D.
Leona Baumgartner, M.D.
Nusret H. Fisek, Ph.D.
Reimert T. Ravenholt, M.D.
Richard H. Schwarz, M.D.

HELPERN: As you know, the fatal infected abortion cases that we saw years ago, before the advent of antibiotics and chemotherapy, are rarely seen today. Most abortion deaths today result from air and chemical embolism, shock, fulminating gas bacillus infection, occasionally tetanus, and improperly administered anesthesia—either intravenous or by inhalation. Overt cases, with perforation of the uterus, shock, hemorrhage, evisceration, and so on, are not so commonly observed as before.

Most of the deaths now are acute and rapid; and, when not suspected by the physician or by the medical examiner or coroner, they are easily overlooked. In jurisdictions in which it is not routinely required that a sudden or medically unattended death without evident violence be reported for official investigation, deaths from illegal abortion often go undetected when an autopsy is performed by an inexperienced or unsuspecting pathologist. The suspicion and recognition of death from abortion are easily obscured by deliberate tampering with or concealment of circumstances in order to make the death seem nonsuspicious or related to some other cause than abortion.

Our first panelist is Dr. Leona Baumgartner.

BAUMGARTNER: I would like to talk about abortion as a public health problem and state that it is one which affects large numbers of people and requires the action of the community to ameliorate it. The individual and his physician cannot handle it alone.

The size of this problem is unknown except in Japan and Eastern Europe. Its complexities—economic, legal, medical, social, religious, and ethical—have been too little studied. There has been too little discussion of these problems among families, professional groups, and in public forums. And yet the quality of family and public life are vitally involved. Scientific research in human sexuality and reproductive physiology has lagged. Methods of abortion are limited.

This situation has characterized other public health problems. One example I would like to make is that of venereal disease. Twenty-five years ago many were embarrassed to discuss the subject. In this country the press refused to print words like *syphilis* or *gonorrhea,* nor could they be used on radio. The size of the problem was pretty well unknown. Police spent fruitless hours trying to find the diseased. Jails, courts, hospitals were crowded with cases. Medical methods and treatment were inadequate and the controls, in general, a farce.

World War II precipitated both public and military interest. Public health, social, and political leaders began to carry on an open and responsible dialogue. The discovery of penicillin made a new era of effective control possible. Public education, new laws to help prevention, and congressional appropriations for federal action against venereal disease followed. New attitudes took over, old taboos were gone.

The importance of a critical mass of public opinion, of open dialogue, of new knowledge, and of scientific discoveries in removing roadblocks to community action, has been demonstrated over and over again.

Closely related to abortion is family planning. Think quickly of the many years of effort which culminated, in 1965, in worldwide action. The climate was right for it. Demographers had gathered the evidence of the dimensions of population growth. Social scientists had tackled attitudes and behavior practices. Research led to the pill and the IUD. The reciprocal relationships between rapid population growth, employment, status of women, other facets of social development, economic growth, and industrialization were recognized. And so the break came.

Viewed in this light, abortion as a public health problem has a long way to go. But signs of change are all around us. The changing world is again forcing action, opening up the necessary dialogue.

I would like to address myself to two questions. What is working for change? Let me name but a few factors: (1) the changing sexual mores of our time; (2) the worldwide rebellion of youth and to a lesser degree perhaps women's rebellion against traditional established ways; (3) the increasing numbers of youth; (4) the rising expectancy for a better life of peoples all over the world; (5) the reexamination by people in the Judeo-Christian religious groups; and (6) the enormous growth of the mass media, with even African and Indian villages affected.

What is needed? (1) More information and research; facts from demographers, epidemiologists, and statisticians; more social and behavioral research so that public and private opinions, beliefs, and behavior, can be more readily changed; (2) more public education on human sexuality and reproduction, economics, sociology, and the human costs of illegal abortion; and (3) more leadership from the health and allied professions.

I would start out with the professionals, because there are professional people at the conference. The American Public Health Association has said: "Abortion is an important means of securing the right to spacing and choosing the number of children wanted. . . . Safe legal abortion should be available to all women." Planned Parenthood-World Population has suggested that all criminal laws regarding abortion should be abolished. I remind you that it was in 1949 that the American Public Health Association was the first professional organization that said something about family planning. It took fifteen years to get to the place where there was enough motivation to do something about it.

We need more education and leadership in legal and legislative halls and more responsibility in ethical and religious circles.

HELPERN: Thank you, Dr. Baumgartner. Our second panelist is Dr. Edwin M. Gold.

GOLD: Until either ideal contraception for family planning becomes universally available and utilized, or legal abortion as a backup method is statutorily provided, or both, illegal abortion will continue to be a major public health problem. The latest estimate of 25 million legal and illegal abortions performed annually, worldwide, was made in 1967 by Professor Karl-Heinz Mehlan of East Germany at the Fifth World Congress of Gynecology and Obstetrics in Sydney, Australia. This is apparently a reasonable estimate.

In 1955, at the Arden House Abortion Conference, it was estimated that between 200,000 and 1.2 million induced abortions per year occurred in the United States. Early in 1968, Michael S. Burnhill, at a meeting of the Population Association of America, projected the frequency of induced abortion in the United States to be between 650,000 and 1.3 million annually. Mehlan stated that in Latin America 50 per cent of pregnancies are currently terminated by illegal abortion. Christopher Tietze reported for Hungary in 1965 a higher legal abortion rate per 1,000 population than the live birth rate, 17.8 and 13.1 respectively.

It is against such a backdrop that we are here to debate the medical ravages consequent to extrahospital abortions. One measure of these ravages is maternal mortality, which is fairly well documented. National vital statistics reveal an 11 per cent decline in puerperal mortality in the United States, from a rate of 3.8 per 10,000 live births in 1958 to 3.4 per 10,000 live births in 1964. During this same period, however, the proportion of maternal deaths due to septic abortion increased from 16 per cent to 21 per cent.

Stevenson's data from the Michigan Maternal Mortality Survey (*Amer. J. Obst. Gynecol.*, *98*:365 [1967]) similarly showed rising maternal mortality rates associated with abortions. For the five-year period 1960 to 1964, 37 per cent of the maternal deaths in Michigan were due to abortion (120 abortion deaths among a total of 321 maternal deaths), whereas in the previous five years, 1955 to 1959, 21 per cent of the maternal deaths were due to abortion.

Further confirmation of the lethal effects of illegal abortion is shown in data from New York City. In the 15 years 1950 to 1964, the percentage of puerperal deaths due to abortion rose from 22.9 per cent to 45.9 per cent.

Fox recently reported on 223 abortion deaths, representing 21 per cent of all maternal deaths studied by the Maternal Mortality Committees of the State of California from August 1957 through December 1965 (*Amer. J. Obst. Gynecol.,* *98*:645 [1967]).

From Turkey came reports that approximately 11,000 married women die each year from abortion.

Professor Mehlan called on the World Health Organization to investigate the world situation, particularly in Latin America, where 50 per cent of pregnancies were terminated by illegal abortions, and four times as many women died as in countries where abortion was legal. He stated, further, that illegal abortion was the world's leading cause of maternal mortality, accounting for 30 to 50 per cent.

Who is the usual victim of fatal abortion? From the mortality data reported in the medical literature, a profile of the victim emerges. She is a 25- to 27-year-old married housewife of lower socioeconomic status, with a median of 3 living children, who has resided for at least 7.5 years in or near a large urban metropolitan area, who has aborted herself or has been aborted by injecting a caustic or toxic solution into her uterus, and was either dead on arrival or lived less than two days after admission to the hospital.

Perhaps of even greater importance than mortality is the continuum of morbidity due to extrahospital or illegal induced abortion. The major cause of this morbidity is infection.

A useful means of indexing the severity of morbidity and the extent of the septic process due to abortion is the classification proposed by Goodno and his co-workers in Baltimore (*Amer. J. Obst. Gynecol., 85*:16 [1963]), as follows: *Type I*: Infection limited to the uterus and its contents. *Type II*: Infection spreading beyond the uterus to involve other pelvic structures. *Type III*: Infection spreading beyond the pelvic structures. On the basis of this classification, Goodno et al. summarized their data as shown in Table 1.

R. Armijo and Mariano Requena in a paper on epidemiological aspects of abortion in Chile, presented at a meeting of the American

Table 1 Three Types of Morbidity Following Abortion

	Type I	Type II	Type III	Total
Number of cases	256	51	35	342
Per cent	74.8	14.9	10.3	100.0
Number admitting interference	34	20	16	70
Per cent admitting interference	13.3	40.0	45.7	20.5
Average time required to reach relatively afebrile status (temperature below 100° F.)	1.5 days	2.7 days	4.7 days	2.0 days
Average total hospital stay	6.1 days	8.4 days	11.0 days	7.0 days
Per cent receiving blood transfusion	42.0	34.0	48.5	41.4

Public Health Association in San Francisco in October 1966, summarized a number of prior reports from Chile as follows: (1) Abortion accounted for 8.1 per cent of all admissions to National Health Service hospitals during the years 1958 to 1960. (2) Abortion accounted for 41.6 per cent of all hospital emergency admissions during that period. (3) Abortion accounted for 26.7 per cent of the total blood transfusions dispensed. (4) In 1960 Chile's National Health Service spent well over one million dollars in hospital care of abortion cases, and it was estimated that in complicated cases the cost of a single survivor was approximately $3,000.

Mojic (*Excerpta Medica*, International Congress series, No. 71, p. 77, 1963), reporting on abortion from Yugoslavia, at the Third European Regional Conference of the International Planned Parenthood Federation in Warsaw in 1962, stated that: (1) With the increase in abortions in Yugoslavia since the abortion laws were liberalized in 1958 and again in 1960, the number of gynecological cases treated in women's dispensaries and hospitals also rose. (2) A fourfold increase in pelvic inflammatory conditions, menstrual disorders, and sterility was noted between the years 1951 and 1960. (3) Of special concern was the 2 to 2½ times increase in hospital admission for extrauterine pregnancies as abortions increased. In certain parts of Yugoslavia nearly every third operation is for extrauterine pregnancy. (4) Published reports from many clinics and hospitals in Yugoslavia confirm the fact that abortion is the main etiological factor in secondary sterility (5,508 cases in 1951; 18,348 in 1960). (5) From the data presented, "the consequences of abortions increase gynecological morbidity and reduce the biological efficiency of women."

From these reports and data that I have so briefly collated, the inescapable conclusion must be drawn that abortion markedly increases gynecological mortality and morbidity, overburdens hospital bed utilization, excessively increases blood transfusion requirements, takes a disproportionately high share of medical cost budgeting, and could in the main be prevented by sound public health programs of sex education and family planning expansion together with rational liberalization of abortion laws enabling legal abortion to serve as an effective backup to contraception.

HELPERN: I am now going to call on Dr. Nusret H. Fisek.

FISEK: I shall talk about abortion in Turkey. Since modern contraceptive methods were unavailable, criminal abortion became a serious public health problem in the late 1950s. The situation was comparable to that in all other countries where socioeconomic development is not accompanied by a reduction in the birth rate by the use of effective contraceptive methods.

Following the suggestions of some leading gynecologists, the Ministry of Health in Turkey established an advisory committee in 1958 in order to study the abortion problem. The committee advised the government to change the existing legal provisions which prohibited the sale and use of contraceptives and the propagation of family-planning knowledge.

The extent of abortions performed and the number of deaths caused in Turkey during the late 1950s and early 1960s are not known exactly. It has been estimated, however, that there were 500,000 abortions and 10,000 deaths due to abortion every year. These figures are derived from Burak's study of 5,000 women admitted to Ankara Maternity Hospital and from a survey carried out in 137 villages in central and western Anatolia by myself and my colleagues. The rates found in these studies were 30 abortions per 100 live births and 6.7 maternal deaths due to abortion per 1,000 live births.

Many women risk their lives in order to terminate unwanted pregnancies. Life is a gift of God to these women. Do we have the right to let them risk their lives? If they do, who is the sinner, we or they? I have heard dozens of shocking stories about criminal abortions, which motivated me to take part in the changing of the policies in Turkey.

Data about hospital abortions are not available in Turkey, but it is known that abortions in hospitals are very limited because it is prohibited by law. Obstetricians who perform abortions for medical reasons, however, are not prosecuted by the attorneys general because the act committed to save a life is not regarded as a crime.

The sale of contraceptives and education of the public in family planning was legalized at the end of a long and difficult struggle in

1955, and abortion for medical reasons in hospitals was legalized in 1967. It is too early to evaluate the results of this change, but a few available observations are encouraging.

The number of abortions (of all kinds) per live births in Ankara hospitals has declined appreciably since 1964. There were 37 abortions per 100 live births in 1964, 28 in 1965, 27 in 1966, and 24 in 1967. The number of maternal deaths due to abortion is around 50 per year. One-third of these deaths are due to abortion with sepsis.

The number of induced abortions is very high despite contraception. For instance, in metropolitan areas, in a study done recently, 56 abortions per 100 live births were reported.

I firmly believe that liberalization of the abortion law does not reduce the criminal abortion rate unless psychosocial reasons are accepted as an excuse for abortion. And most physicians do not approve of doing abortions for these reasons.

HELPERN: Now I am going to call upon Dr. Richard H. Schwarz.

SCHWARZ: As an obstetrician-gynecologist charged with supervision of the care of a large number of postabortion patients both in a municipal hospital and in the University of Pennsylvania Hospital, I should like to make several observations on the current problems concerning abortions.

Whether there be 200,000 or 1,500,000 abortions per year and whether the deaths from abortion are 500 or 5,000, the consequences of these abortions still comprise a major health hazard. Abortion complications in Philadelphia account for up to 50 per cent of pregnancy-related deaths.

There has been, in our experience, a significant reduction in the total number of such postabortion patients admitted to our hospitals in recent years and perhaps an even more striking reduction in abortion-related deaths. The reasons are multiple.

First of all, there has been a remarkable decrease in the total number of deliveries occuring in municipal hospitals. This reduction at the Philadelphia General Hospital is between 40 and 50 per cent in the past five years. This is in part a result of the overall slow-down in the birth rate attributable to dissemination of contraceptive information and material. But it is also in great part due to redistribution of the responsibility for medical care of the disadvantaged. Developments such as the Maternal-Infant Care program have relocated many of the municipal hospital patients into the private community hospitals.

Since these patients receive obstetrical care in this new setting, the same group are, in increasing numbers, finding postabortal care there and, in some instances, also in the office of the private practitioner. I believe we have an educational problem, for the critically ill postabortion patient may present a great clinical challenge to the physician infrequently exposed to these cases.

The decrease in abortion deaths is also significant in our institution. From 1955 to 1965 we had two to four such deaths per year and in the past three years we have had none. The reasons for this are clear. We have learned better how to manage these patients. An aggressive approach to completion of the very septic abortion and an expanded understanding of the pathogenesis of shock due to sepsis and how to manage it are but a few of the advances responsible.

Unfortunately, as in the case of contraception, the greatest reduction in the number of extrahospital abortions has not been in the hard-core indigent group. This same group which is most difficult to reach with contraception continues to have the crude, generally foreign-body-induced abortions, many self-induced, all amateurish, with a high incidence of sepsis.

I hope that changes will come which will one day eliminate this cause, not only of death, but of horrendous morbidity. Until this happens, however, the obstetrician-gynecologist faces a continuing challenge to his clinical proficiency.

HELPERN: Our last panelist is Dr. Reimert T. Ravenholt.

RAVENHOLT: As Director of Population for the Agency for International Development, I am concerned with developing as rapidly as possible a program of assistance to the family-planning programs of the developing countries. I firmly believe that abortion will play a very important role in these programs.

A key judgment often heard is that the full implementation of family-planning programs and the full exercise of fertility control by women and couples everywhere will fall far short of the goal of zero population growth because knowledge, attitude, and practice studies have shown that women want too many children. But this judgment appears to be based on the simple assumption that the composite response of all women of reproductive age and experience to such a question as "What do you consider the ideal number of children?" bears close and reliable relationship to the number of children women would have, if they reproduced only if and when they wished from menarche to menopause. This assumption is not supported by logic or definitive fact.

Bearing and rearing children is hard work and few women have unlimited enthusiasm for the task. If given the choice each month of whether they wish to be pregnant, many considerations other than ultimate family size would guide their reproductive behavior. For many women postponement of pregnancy means reduction in completed family size.

The current large excess of births over deaths in many developing countries has generated some pessimism concerning the collective wisdom of people individually exercising freedom of choice. But on the other hand there appears to be a sound basis for optimism. The pattern seems clear that in those countries where women need not reproduce except if and when they choose—meaning they have access to the hindsight method of abortion as well as the foresight method of contraception—the situation is encouraging.

In Japan and several countries of Eastern Europe the net reproduction rate has fallen below one. Social concern has then shifted from the problem of too great a reproductive rate to concern over the possibility of too low a reproductive rate.

I think that this whole concept of foresight methods of birth control verses hindsight methods is very important. We already have excellent methods of foresight control. But, unfortunately, many people, especially those of low economic and educational status, both in this country and abroad, lack sufficient foresight to accomplish their fertility control entirely by this means. The matter of access to hindsight methods is all-important in striving for the goal that every child be wanted and well cared for.

We have tried, in thinking about how we might allocate funds for research, to define what would be the ideal means of fertility control, if we could develop it. My preference would be for a nontoxic and completely effective substance which, when self-administered by women on a single occasion, would insure nonpregnancy at the completion of one monthly cycle.

Some people prefer to think of the ideal fertility-control agent as very long-acting—something that you would take in one injection for six or nine months' protection. I believe that the ideal method will always be related to the monthly cycle. I would suggest that in abortions performed under favorable circumstances we have a method that comes very close to this ideal. It really conforms to the ideal, as I have defined it, with the exception of self-administration.

Much has been said here about the public health hazards of abortion, but from where I sit the hazards of nonabortion are much greater. In this country unwanted children are surely a far greater public health burden and menace than is abortion. This is also true for the developing countries. The public health problem generated by the lack of access to abortion and birth control, leading to excess population growth, is far greater than the problem of abortion.

HELPERN: Table 2 lists the number of abortion deaths in New York City between 1918 and 1967. To my knowledge, only one of these deaths resulted from therapeutic abortion in a hospital.

Table 2 Abortion Deaths Investigated by Office of Chief Medical Examiner from 1918 to 1967*

1918 – 130	1931 – 140	1943 – 33	1955 – 34
1919 – 127	1932 – 105	1944 – 29	1956 – 35
1920 – 118	1933 – 122	1945 – 31	1957 – 33
1921 – 144	1934 – 105	1946 – 23	1958 – 41
1922 – 107	1935 – 100	1947 – 32	1959 – 38
1923 – 131	1936 – 92	1948 – 20	1960 – 46
1924 – 127	1937 – 82	1949 – 23	1961 – 58
1925 – 112	1938 – 74	1950 – 25	1962 – 53
1926 – 118	1939 – 53	1951 – 15	1963 – 41
1927 – 124	1940 – 70	1952 – 23	1964 – 34
1928 – 107	1941 – 48	1953 – 35	1965 – 39
1929 – 118	1942 – 36	1954 – 31	1966 – 30
1930 – 89			1967 – 20

*There were 21 such deaths in 1968. [Editor's note.]

I might say we have a fairly high rate of discovery in New York City. The opportunity of obscuring an abortion death is very unlikely. We have a very effective Health Department, which screens all the death certificates, and anything unusual would be referred to us, particularly in a woman of childbearing age.

ABORTION AND PSYCHIATRY

The Effect of Abortion upon Psychic Equilibrium and Vice Versa

Theodore Lidz, M.D. (moderator)
Harold Rosen, Ph.D., M.D. (rapporteur)
Leon Eisenberg, M.D.
Jerome M. Kummer, M.D.
Robert W. Laidlaw, M.D.
Natalie Shainess, M.D.
Robert B. White, M.D.

T. LIDZ: Psychiatry makes 95 per cent of the decisions about legal abortion in most states. No other medical discipline seems amorphous enough to fit its decisions into the restrictive forms forced upon us. Perhaps this is because psychiatry is more willing than other disciplines to think of the emotional well-being of the mother and the future of the fetus. It considers these its responsibility.

Questions arise. What are psychiatric indications for abortion? Are there psychiatric contraindications? We are bounded by dangers due to continuation of the pregnancy and birth of the child, and dangers from illegal abortion. We are concerned with what must be given to the child by mother, family, and society if that child is to develop into an emotionally healthy, well-functioning individual. What limits will be set in an overpopulated world upon those who bear children, what kind of children will they give rise to, and what type of rearing will these children receive?

I would like to call upon Dr. Robert B. White to state his views.

WHITE: In 1966 I attempted to clarify my thoughts about the psychiatric implications of induced abortion through discussions with colleagues in psychiatry, obstetrics, religion, and law. I found a bewildering clutter of diverse but strongly held opinions. The literature reflects this. Bolter, for example, in 1962 stated that a threat of suicide is the only proper psychiatric indication for abortion. He added that he had never seen a patient without guilt from previous therapeutic or illegal abortion. But in 1963 Jerome M.

Kummer, who polled thirty-two experienced psychiatrists, found that three-quarters of them had never seen a patient with moderate or severe psychiatric sequelae from induced abortion; the remainder had rarely observed any.

Three main factors cause most of this confusion:

1. There is a lack of systematic, properly gathered data on the effect on the woman of being either granted or refused an abortion.

2. Men (physicians, clergy, lawmakers), not women, have the predominant voice in setting policies and laws governing abortion, and the abortion issue tends to evoke in men powerful unconscious conflicts and motivations. These conflicts impair rational judgment and decisions.

3. The problem is usually considered simultaneously from a variety of viewpoints—scientific, legal, and theological. If we, as physicians, can find sound scientific information on the many unanswered questions concerning the emotional impact of induced abortion, many of our arguments with our legal and theological colleagues can be avoided.

Most of the medical and psychiatric literature consists of anecdotal case histories or statistical surveys that lack depth and precision. Most fail to emphasize the crucial psychiatric question, namely, the motivational systems that prompt a woman to seek or accept abortion. A woman's emotional response to an induced abortion depends in great measure on her conscious and unconscious motives for seeking it; on her conscious and unconscious feelings toward the pregnancy, the father of the baby, herself, and the physician who performs the abortion; and upon the emotional tone of the context in which she receives it. Detailed and extensive study of these factors is needed. Follow-up questionnaire or single interview studies can not give us the data we need. A few cases would be most helpful if studied in depth by a psychoanalytically trained observer in continuous contact with the patient from the moment the question of abortion comes under medical consideration till a year or two afterward.

Psychotherapists, including psychoanalysts, have had patients who obtain abortions during therapy. Retrospective data about these merits systematic collecting. Similar studies in depth are needed of women who genuinely want abortion but do not receive it. How do such pregnancies proceed? What is the quality of the relation of mother to infant? How does the relation of mother to offspring develop in the early years of childhood?

Medical, legal, and theological opposition to easing restrictions on abortion is intense; we must therefore assume powerful unconscious motives for this. Do similar motives becloud the objectivity of observers who try to answer the question of what the emotional impacts are on a woman who has an abortion?

Again and again, as we read the literature with respect to this, the male physician seems to fear granting a woman a greater say in whether she will or will not keep a pregnancy. I think pregnancy symbolizes proof of male potency. If men grant women the right to dispose of that proof whenever they want to, we men feel terribly threatened lest women rob us of our potency and our masculinity at will.

If a woman seeks an abortion because husband, boyfriend, mother, or mother-in-law has talked her into it, she may later suffer grief and depression or hate those who push her to seek what in her inner motivation she opposes. But I agree with Helena Deutsch's assertion that "a motherly woman, who finds sufficient gratifications for her motherliness in her previously born children, reacts to the loss [through abortion] rationally, that is to say, without further emotional complications."

Any woman who, upon adequate reflection and with opportunity to explore her feelings with a sympathetic physician, wants to terminate her pregnancy because of a significant threat to her welfare or her family's welfare from physical, emotional, social, or financial problems, should be granted that abortion, provided such counseling shows that her conclusion is thoughtful and considered, and provided further that an adequate plan can be worked out for follow-up consultative help so she can cope with later conflicts.

I am speaking of abortion during the first three months or so of pregnancy. As Dr. John Howells pointed out in 1968, the pregnant woman has no meaningful image of a fetus within her prior to the beginning of its movement. But with quickening, the infant-to-be becomes a reality to her. Destroying that being now has vastly different emotional consequences from removing an embryo that she does not yet consider a real being.

T. LIDZ: Thank you. I think we should hear now from Dr. Natalie Shainess.

SHAINESS: Christopher Tietze has noted the relation of tolerance of abortion to political desires for increased or decreased populations. Robert Hall, Harold Rosen, and Lawrence Lader have stressed hypocritical attitudes in our society to abortion. Robert Laidlaw and Peck have suggested that the dangers, physical and mental, of therapeutic abortion have been exaggerated and are more often the consequences of self-induced or illegal abortion. John Howells considers the woman's needs as a major determinant, and points to our inconsistent attitude of planning for a wanted pregnancy while refusing abortion for the unwanted. Robert White notes that some male attitudes reflect the male's own psychosexual problems. Theodore ·Lidz has observed that serious reactions to abortion are fewer than to unwanted pregnancy, while Laidlaw noted that many adverse reactions to abortion result from the devastating circumstances of illegal abortion. In my experience quests for abortion often take on the fantastic Kafkaesque quality of *The Castle* or *The Trial*, and ego-damaging consequences are more extensive than generally realized.

Peck asks if a woman has a right to decide whether to give birth, and if legal abortion has a role in population control. Both questions can be answered in the affirmative but are antithetical; the first raises the issue of ethical concern for woman, the second is related to expediency.

The role of the father is largely neglected. He is an equal partner in procreation, and he often has the major share of the pleasure with virtually no responsibility. This is obvious in rape, but the complex uses by humans of sexual intercourse relate to married life as well. All are aware that refusal of abortion in some instances perpetuates exceptional outrages (rape and fetal malformation, for example). But it is to the less dramatic, more run-of-the-mill but nonetheless painful and unbearable (the pun is intended) unwelcome pregnancies that I wish to direct attention, and to the consequences for society as well as for woman and family. I want to encircle in red— the color of the blood of women crucified by prevailing and predominantly male attitudes—the immaturity, irrationality, and inconsistency of so many of our conventional ethical, moral, legal, and religious concepts.

That woman has accepted her secondary position derives in good measure, early in history, from her relatively physical weakness in relation to the male, her vulnerability to rape, and her more or less perpetual state of pregnancy. These served the species' survival, as did woman's greater durability, but the latter has in no way lent support to her own causes. Impregnation is an accident of nature that then shapes the life of the mother. This accident is often in conflict with her needs and strivings.

Human beings continually alter nature. Yet in regard to abortion, and to a lesser extent contraception, not only has the effort to deal with chance been deemed impermissible, but a series of rationalizations has been constructed to bolster prevailing attitudes with dire predictions of guilt and damage to the woman. I have never seen an instance of genuine guilt or regret after abortion—perhaps because I have not conveyed expectation of it. I have seen great relief. I have seen the desperate suicidal chances women take to obtain abortion, and I have seen a worsening of the marital relationship where abortion could not be obtained. I have heard a few a priori expressions of guilt, but believe them to be fearful and distorted statements of other and complex dynamics.

There are at least three types of out-of-wedlock pregnancies. The most disturbed girls become pregnant to live out a parthenogenetic fantasy, with the child serving as the girl's only connection with the world. Is it wise to let such girls become mothers? Then there are girls "caught" by mischance who, although relatively healthy, cannot bear becoming victims of circumstance. The third group is from a socioeconomic subculture indifferent to marital status.

Pregnancy may be a symptom of emotional ill health. In such cases, the girl or woman is usually insistent on having the child. The initial reaction to discovery of an unwelcome pregnancy, on the other hand, is surprise, disbelief, anger, desperation. Threats of suicide are more real than generally supposed, and suicides more frequent. I know of several instances in which only the woman knew of the pregnancy, desperate and devious efforts at obtaining illegal abortion failed, and suicide was attempted—by auto accident in two cases. Possibly some will to live prevented major disasters; but, had they died, who would have suspected suicide because of pregnancy?

As the pregnancy progresses suicidal thoughts, depression, and a gamut of other psychiatric disorders appear. A major psychosomatic expression of rejection is vomiting—a symbolic effort to vomit the pregnancy out—and this may become pernicious. Hypertensive responses and preeclampsia are also somatic expressions of rejection.

In the third trimester, a calmer psychological state seems to prevail. The fact of pregnancy is well established; it is known to all, so that the social group has been "informed." The woman is, to quote Rilke, "weighted down by the fruit of her body" and has little energy for protest. Most statistical surveys show fewer psychotic breakdowns at this time. But shortly after delivery serious trouble may occur. The biphasic curve of brief euphoria and slump into depression, always present in the early postpartum period, may herald anything from mild depression to delirious excitement and ultimate schizophrenic and paranoid responses. One patient spoke of herself as being paralyzed by polio, a symbolic or metaphoric statement of the harm done to her by the fetus and of her inability to care for the baby. Some women give their infants up for adoption and a series of foster homes—a disadvantaged start in life. Others relentlessly express their rejection and sometimes hatred through their maternal dynamics in relation to the child. Lidz and Jules Henry have documented this through their studies of families of schizophrenic children.

Unwelcome pregnancy results in a foredoomed child. Refusal to permit abortion results in unfortunate and disturbed children. Ultimately, seeding an already hostile, overcrowded society with unfortunates such as these distorts potentially more satisfactory feminine lives and furthers inadequacy, hostility, and destructiveness within our society.

Howells has observed, as have I, that before quickening, the fetus is not a reality, not a child, to the woman. This is when she should have ready access to abortion and this should be a matter between the woman and her physician or the clinic. Hospitals and contraceptive clinics should have trained social workers, if psychiatrists are not available, to discuss personal issues without bias so that women may be clearer about their feelings and motivations before taking action, and so that they may also have a chance to air their feelings afterwards.

Men must commit themselves to their responsibility for abortion. Let them be unable to ask blithely, "What will women choose, the incubator or the incinerator?" Rather, let them ask, "How can a woman raging against a pregnancy be a devoted wife and good mother?" or "What is the effect upon a woman, when the sometimes expressed fantasy—fear in pregnancy of creating a monster—a reflection of damaged ego—may be augmented by the certainty of fetal malformation?" What is the effect upon a woman of harboring the dark secret of hating a child which has been forced upon her?

What is good preventive psychiatry? Our society devotes tremendous effort and expense to the physically and mentally handicapped. It is time for measures that free us to aid the healthy and encourage the gifted. Let us educate men to responsibility and women to proper use and mastery of their reproductive function. Let us espouse the philosophy of John Dewey in encouraging development rather than stultifying by restriction and punishment.

T. LIDZ: Dr. Shainess, would you change "unwelcome" to "unwanted"? Many unwelcome pregnancies are accepted.

SHAINESS: "Unwanted" to me implies a previous state of mind on the part of the woman. "Unwelcome" to me implies an event to which the mother responds.

ROSEN: I have seen a number of pregnancies, wanted and even planned at first but unwelcome on various levels, for which we recommended abortion.

T. LIDZ: Dr. Eisenberg, would you comment now?

L. EISENBERG: I agree with the conclusions of both Doctors White and Shainess, but not with their logic or their reasons. They have not made clear what studies they feel necessary.

With psychiatric studies, for example, of adopted children, what comparison or control group would be adequate? Normal children biologically reared by their own adequate families? Foster children? Can adopted children be compared with foster children kicked around in some home or other?

We need to study women who are pregnant because they wish to be pregnant, and we need to study unwillingly pregnant women, some of whom will have an abortion and some of whom will not. For this there should be a comparison group of nonpregnant women. What about concern about parity, about time frequency with which pregnancies occur, about reasons why abortions are granted or refused? Studies like these imply a major twenty-year undertaking.

Guilt is so pervasive that people can pin it on almost anything. It can be based on previous "unnatural thoughts" about an animal, on thoughts of sex, or on an abortion twenty years previously. Abortion is convenient to focus guilt on because the mores of our society make it so. It will be less convenient once we have changed our mores.

Doctors White, Shainess, and I are in agreement on the need for abortion for any woman who has thought through and reasonably understands the consequences after one, two, or three psychiatric interviews. This is the time limit we have within which to operate.

I write letters recommending abortion that are frankly fraudulent, because I am satisfied to be used so that someone may obtain what our society otherwise would deny to her. But data for psychiatric indications, as they are usually discussed, are difficult to elicit. Will an abortion prevent or lessen the possibility of psychosis, for instance? One can of course extract from a cooperative patient a statement about contemplation of suicide. But issues we deal with here are issues of humanity, of the role of physicians and of women in society. If psychiatrists are to be missionaries, to make this change, I am delighted to cooperate, but when I do I am using the term "psychiatry" in a sense not ordinarily used in medical circles.

T. Lidz: Thank you, Dr. Eisenberg. Dr. Laidlaw?

Laidlaw: In thirty years of experience, I have never seen any significant psychiatric aftermath of an abortion arranged in the therapeutic setting. I cannot say this about illegal abortions.

One woman who was met on a dark corner, blindfolded, and driven to a dark part of town, told me ten years later that ever since she had had what in the military we called battle dreams. She would wake with a start, shuddering and cringing in the middle of the night, hearing in her mind the scraping of the pail as it dragged across the tile floor.

The psychiatrist has a role to play in preventing even minor disturbances after abortion. If he is seeing his patient for the first time, while taking her history he should support and nonjudgmentally reassure her. She often has no idea of what an abortion is like, of the fact that it is essentially minor surgery, and that she will have good anesthesia and make a quick recovery. For the first time she may now be able to realize what lies ahead.

In my part of the country, two psychiatrists are necessary. I make sure that I call in a colleague who feels as I do, and I call him before he sees the patient. Then, if the patient has not been referred by a gynecologist, I refer her to one who takes time enough to get to know her. Too many merely give her an appointment for the operating room at a certain time. A warm, supportive, and understanding attitude is important as a buildup to the procedure itself. And my letter of recommendation to the hospital abortion board assures the patient that the board will not violate her confidences.

As Dr. Eisenberg stated, in many cases we must go out on a limb to find some indication which fits in with existing laws. But we can always say that the patient is depressed and that if her pregnancy continues, this depression may become severe and even assume suicidal proportions; an abortion committee under most circumstances will then allow abortion for a case that does not strictly fall within the present code.

The psychiatrist can help his patient when she goes into the hospital. I always try to see her preoperatively there. And I keep a list of nurses whose reactions to patients I know. On the nursing floor and in the operating room there may be a few cold and hostile nurses, usually Roman Catholic, and the patient should be protected and isolated from these women during her short hospital stay.

Then after the operation, when I see her again, I talk in terms not of *delivery* but of *deliverance*. This is a time for rejoicing. Occasionally psychiatric follow-up is indicated, not so much because of a guilt reaction but because the patient needs help in working out her other life problems.

I feel that the psychiatrist has an opportunity to practice preventive medicine here just as he sees to the welfare of his patient all the way through any therapeutic procedure.

T. Lidz: Dr. Laidlaw has emphasized two points that have been of great concern to us in our hospital: the difficulty of having the gynecologist, particularly on the ward service, notify the psychiatrist when the patient is coming in; and secondly, the problems posed by nurses antagonistic to the patient.

Dr. Kummer, will you comment at this time?

Kummer: We have a societal schizophrenia when it comes to abortion. Rigid laws, rigid restrictions against people following natural instincts for self-preservation and preservation of the family, rigid restrictions against physicians who practice their profession to the best of their ability in the best interests of their patients—this, to my way of thinking, is a schizophrenic attitude. It is within the province of psychiatrists interested in social psychiatry to attempt to point out such schizophrenic thinking and action when we see it and to deal with the resistances on whatever level we are able to.

Apropos of this, Dr. Lidz asked us to consider psychiatric indications and contraindications to abortion. The time has long since passed for this. Most psychiatrists take many factors into account, weighing them carefully, just as an obstetrician considering a cesarean section does, balancing pros with cons before reaching his decision. We try to help our patient weigh the many factors in her condition to arrive at a decision concerning her pregnancy that is valid for her and her family.

Any woman wanting an abortion should be entitled to it after she has had a chance to discuss and explore it more fully with trusted counsel, whether psychiatrist or family counselor or obstetrician.

T. Lidz: If abortion is freely available at the request of the woman, does a psychiatrist have to be involved in the judgment?

Rosen: If a psychistrist, in the opinion of the referring physician, is needed to handle an emotional problem of his patient's, then a psychiatrist should be called in, whether the referring physician be a surgeon considering an appendectomy, an internist treating a patient in heart failure, or a gynecologist seeing a woman who wishes an abortion. But not otherwise.

KUMMER: I am in complete agreement. However, I would like to encourage one or two preabortal counseling sessions with obstetricians trained to listen to patients, and also a postabortal counseling session, so the woman can air some of her feelings and not build up a pressure of guilt.

T. LIDZ: Dr. Geijerstam, what is the situation in Sweden?

GEIJERSTAM: We presuppose consultation by the woman with a physician. We do not have abortion on demand in Sweden.

A social worker should be the first to take care of the woman in order to give her the social support she may need. It is my impression as an obstetrician that the woman who asks for an abortion is often extremely ambivalent, and she needs both social and personal support to make this choice intelligently.

The situation is different in the various trimesters of pregnancy. For instance, the obstetrician is involved in only the first stage of the two-stage procedure used later in pregnancy, and for him this is a depersonalized experience. He is not involved in the actual abortion. The woman is either by herself then or with personnel who are not prepared to take care of her during this very trying situation.

T. LIDZ: Dr. Cernoch, would you comment about the situation in Czechoslovakia?

CERNOCH: What can I say? We have observed some complications. We have seen two or three suicides before abortion. But we have also observed two or three suicides afterwards. These were not because of the unwanted pregnancy, but because of the factors that made the pregnancy unwanted.

POMEROY: Dr. Laidlaw, when differentiating between therapeutic and illegal abortions, was making a plea for the quality of abortion experience. If the ward nurse is against it, a woman may have a better experience with an illegal than a therapeutic abortion.

KUMMER: In the book by Gebhardt and yourself, you pointed out that even with back-alley abortions there are very few adverse psychological reactions.

POMEROY: The incidence is about 14 per cent.

ASHER: Dr. Eisenberg, what studies, psychological tests, and in-depth interviews would you envision to gather the kind of information you and Dr. White think should be studied?

L. EISENBERG: I am less interested in collecting scientific data than in abolishing an absurd social custom. To wait on scientific data condemns women to increasingly difficult times. It is absurd to require that each woman see a psychiatrist, if only because of the lack of psychiatrists and the even greater lack of those with a decent point of view.

ROSSI: In New Haven, Boston, Los Angeles, Chicago, and San Francisco you psychiatrists have no difficulty finding an obstetrician to whom you can refer a woman for this kind of compassionate handling and assistance, but what about the woman in Alabama, in Milwaukee, or in smaller towns elsewhere? How can she find an obstetrician at this time? In the projected future will we have a new generation of obstetricians with this compassion?

WHITE: Public opinion and legal opinion are shifting. Medical opinion is shifting. Within three to five years, almost all states will have something like the statute recommended by the American Law Institute. But for abortion to be between woman and physician, we need to get systematic data in a ten- or fifteen-year project. The law will not be changed in many states.

KUMMER: Some day we will have a law in the United States completely legalizing abortion.

Rosen: In some one state within the next few years—and then in all the states!

Shainess: We must do studies, I suppose, but I agree with Dr. Eisenberg. Let's not wait.

Potter, Klein, and Dick a dozen years ago in a study of unwelcome pregnancies found that, as pregnancies advance and up to a year after delivery, the idea of motherhood became accepted or tolerated. But this conclusion depended on how they interpreted what the women under study said.

Viola Bernard and Mark Flapan, in a study of infertile women, devised a variety of ingenious tests for unconscious as well as conscious material. Apparently unsophisticated women, some of whom loudly protested that they wanted children, actually did not. One test, for example, involved the women's playing with a doll as if they were caring for a baby. All kinds of pathology manifested itself in their actions and in their comments. They would say, "I want to have a baby," but when asked, "How come?" would answer, "Because otherwise my husband will leave me for another woman." In terms of positive desire for maternity, this leaves much open to question.

T. Lidz: Dr. Rosen is the anchor man for this panel. He will summarize or supplement our comments.

Rosen: I should like to comment about the last hundred pregnancies that were interrupted on my recommendation. They involved 107 girls. The pregnancies in two-thirds of the cases were between the 16th and 22d week. There were no untoward physical sequelae. Two did have adverse emotional reactions. One had to have ten and the other thirty hours of concentrated, intensive psychiatric treatment immediately after the abortion to prevent psychotic decompensation. Both are now under treatment by psychiatrists in their home communities.

Laidlaw: Were these two patients previously disturbed?

Rosen: They were disturbed previously and had been in psychiatric treatment. It was felt in advance that florid psychotic symptoms might be precipitated if they were aborted. They were referred to us for this reason.

Another girl we saw had been aborted after a single consultation session by a psychiatrist. He felt that there was no problem involved at all. She is at present under treatment by another psychiatrist. She had deliberately arranged to get pregnant to get away from her fear of homosexuality. As it later developed she was postabortally arranging to conceive again to keep from facing her homosexuality on conscious levels. There should in advance have been more extensive psychiatric evaluation and treatment so that postabortally this girl would not have had to be seen as an emergency because she was developing a homosexual panic. This could have been foreseen. With some girls a single psychiatric consultation session is not nearly enough.

Forcing a girl to carry an unwelcome and unwanted pregnancy resentfully to term cannot possibly be helpful to her emotional well-being or to that of her family. A psychiatric problem, if we consider the situation from this angle, is always present. Psychiatrically, if a girl is reactively anxiety-ridden or even, perhaps only mildly, reactively depressed, this is sufficient indication for interrupting an unwanted and resented pregnancy. With abortion she will then regain her prepregnancy emotional status.

I do not feel that a woman should be referred for psychiatric consultation merely because she happens to wish an abortion. If she is thought to be emotionally ill, then but only then, she should be referred for psychiatric consultation. At present, in most cases she must see one psychiatrist. Too many hospitals then compel her to see a second psychiatrist. She feels she is forced to plead her cause to both. Her socially inculcated guilt is intensified.

A number of hospitals, in addition to this, require a notarized certificate from her stating that she wants the abortion and her reasons for wanting it. This makes it still worse. She must then wait on all the rigmarole of abortion board proceedings with all the anxiety attendant on them, not knowing if her request will be granted or not. This drives her guilt still deeper. Administrative procedures like these are sadistic. They have nothing to do with the practice of medicine or of the specialties of obstetrics and psychiatry.

ABORTION AND OBSTETRICS

The Means of Determining the Legitimacy of Requests for Abortion

Louis M. Hellman, M.D. (moderator)
Curtis J. Lund, M.D. (rapporteur)
Irvin M. Cushner, M.D.
Alan F. Guttmacher, M.D.
Octavio Rodrigues-Lima, M.D.
Edmund W. Overstreet, M.D.
Clyde Randall, M.D.

HELLMAN: This panel has been asked to consider how best to evaluate requests for abortion. The answer to this question must, of course, depend upon the type of abortion laws we have. Suppose, for example, that we lived in a society where there were no restrictions of any kind and where any woman could walk into a hospital or a doctor's office, ask for an abortion, and get one. This immediately supposes a radical departure from standard medical practice. Today you cannot even walk into a doctor's office and ask for nose drops. If he is a good doctor, he will ask you what is the matter and he will take a history and look in your nose before deciding on the right kind of treatment. But we must admit at the beginning that a request for abortion is slightly different from the requests for other health care. It has overtones perhaps not germane to health care in general.

There is another problem touched on tangentially today, but I think of great concern to many of us, namely that if there were no restrictions on obtaining abortion the practice of obstetrics would be largely taken up with the performance of abortion. Whether this is a scare threat or whether it is real I have no idea.

So let us address ourselves to the legitimacy, not only of practices as they are today, but of practices as they might be if not for most of the restrictions. I have asked Dr. Guttmacher to start this panel session, and then we will go around the table. As far as I know, and I have done no research on this, he developed the committee approach which is both the anathema and the boon of many of us who practice medicine today.

GUTTMACHER: My discussion has to be somewhat autobiographical, and I apologize. I got my medical training in Baltimore at Johns Hopkins and completed the residency in 1929. We had a very powerful professor of obstetrics. Nobody made decisions about anything except Dr. Williams. There was never an abortion committee and never a discussion. The professor made all the decisions and I may say he made them quite honestly and usually very well. My confidence in this unilateral type of decision was somewhat shaken when one of my colleagues came to me for an abortion for his wife and I could not see any possible justification for it, although I was very sympathetic with his problem. Later I learned that his wife was aborted on the grounds of malnutrition by the chief of gynecology at another hospital. I began to think that putting the power of the Supreme Court in one man was probably not very wise.

When I became chief of obstetrics at Mt. Sinai Hospital in Baltimore, I rather enjoyed this kind of sovereignty over my staff in which I decided whether there would be abortion or no abortion. Then I thought about it a little more maturely and decided that this was not right. First of all, I had the tendency to bend backward with my more intimate friends and bend forward with my less intimate friends. This seemed rather irrational and I decided, therefore, that this should be a judicial decision made by a combination of medical disciplines. I assembled a committee consisting of the chief of obstetrics, who was the chairman of the committee, and a senior attending in medicine, surgery, pediatrics, and psychiatry. This then became the abortion board and it decided on all cases.

When I came to Mt. Sinai Hospital in New York I again established a board and as far as I know they still have it. It operated in the same way and met every Wednesday afternoon at five o'clock. We required a letter from the obstetrician and a letter from the consultant stating why this abortion should be performed. Then the obstetrician came and presented his case before the committee. We had the privilege of having the consultant present the case and any other consultant we wished. Then the committee would decide. It was hospital policy to have a unanimous decision. Occasionally, there was a difference of opinion, but this was rather rare.

The committee almost eliminated the differential between the ward and the private patient. I have before me statistics which I compiled from 1953 to 1960, during which time we had an incidence of 6.3 therapeutic abortions per 1,000 live births on the private service and 4.6 on the clinic service. There is a difference of 1.7 per thousand births between these two services. This difference is due not to discrimination but to the fact that the ward patient presents herself considerably later in pregnancy than does the private patient. My residents understood that abortion was just as proper and easy to obtain (or difficult to obtain) for the ward patient as the private patient. They were encouraged to bring cases to the committee just as readily as the private practitioner. Unfortunately, in most institutions the board system decreases the incidence of abortion. I think it did that at Mt. Sinai, judging by the lessened incidence of abortion when the board came into being. From that point of view perhaps it is a backward step. On the other hand, it does iron out some of the inequalities of one man making decisions alone.

ROEMER: Do you think, perhaps, that thirty-eight years ago the board system was a sound innovation and that now the situation has changed because of new attitudes and greater experiences?

GUTTMACHER: Actually, the system was started in 1945, so it was twenty-three years ago. I think we have learned a lot since then. At that time there was a contest to show the lowest incidence of therapeutic abortion.

HELLMAN: Let's move a little bit further, then we will come back to your question. Dr. Overstreet?

OVERSTREET: Having known Dr. Guttmacher all these years, I had not realized that it was he who forced upon us the committee system. At the present time we are forced by law to operate under it in California. I would like to mention briefly some of the problems we are encountering under this state law committee system. Fortunately, the definition of statutory rape is easy in California. It is 14 years or under and all you need to prove it is a birth certificate for the girl. Why the cut-off point comes at 14 rather than at 15, 16, or 17 still remains an open question. Forcible rape is a problem at the present time in California because the presentation of false rape cases has increased. This is evidenced by the fact that among the applications for therapeutic abortion for forcible rape in California, 19 per cent were turned down by the committee in terms of their disbelief in the actuality of the forcible rape itself. Our biggest problem, of course, is in the area of therapeutic abortion for mental health. First of all, the definitions as stated by the law are so extraordinarily vague that it becomes necessary for the committees to interpret them and to set down guidelines. The California law states that mental health must be impaired to such a degree that the patient "is dangerous to herself or to the person or property of others, or is in need of supervision or restraint." How do you define supervision? Is it supervision every day? Supervision by whom? Does a single consultation constitute supervision? This is a very difficult interpretation which we have to make. Whether we like it or not, it has to be made under this specific statute. Under it, psychiatrists will vary greatly in their diagnosis of mental illness and the nonpsychiatric physician finds it even more difficult to decide whether or not a patient has mental illness to the point of justifying therapeutic abortion. Should the nonpsychiatric members of the committee accept the statement of a psychiatrist that the patient is mentally ill or is it incumbent upon them to form their own judgment? Many of our committees are worried about the question of "serious intent to procure a criminal abortion." Does this constitute self-destruction or self-dangerous behavior within the intent of the law? Some committees feel that it does. Other committees feel it does not.

In trying to make a reasonably honest decision about whether we are dealing with a true mental illness, we sought desperately for help from sources other than our own committee. One thing we are doing with our therapeutic abortion committee at the University of California is to see whether the MMPI will be of any help to us in deciding whether a patient has mental illness of this degree. This work is being carried out by Dr. Davidson from the department of psychiatry there. Of 66 cases studied, 52 per cent by the MMPI showed psychotic symptomatology, 29 per cent showed neurotic symptomatology, and only 18 per cent of the results were indeterminate by this test. Actually, while we don't depend on the MMPI to make a decision, it has been very helpful in borderline cases.

Still, the adjudication of therapeutic abortion, especially the mental illness area (and that is 88 per cent of our cases at the present time), is uneven, inequitable, and discriminatory. No one is happy about it in California. No satisfactory guidelines are developing as to how to approach candidates for therapeutic abortion. Several studies going on now in California, and some of the Swedish results, suggest that forcing a woman to carry an unwanted pregnancy to term against her will always impairs her mental health. If this is true it would probably make further changes unnecessary for those states that have mental health in the statutes. It would make committee work much simpler. It would only be a matter of determining whether the pregnancy is truly unwanted. It would go far toward solving the problem of criminal abortion, which in our experience this new law is not doing in California. It would satisfy the increasing demand for abolition of compulsory pregnancy and at the same time, of course, it would raise tremendous practical problems by greatly increasing the number of therapeutic abortions.

BURNHILL: I think the abortion committee has become a judiciary committee to interpret the law. Someday some committee will be taken to task and the lawyers will argue about the interpretation of the terms. They are liable to come out with an entirely different interpretation. I think the courts, not the committees, should adjudicate the law.

HELLMAN: I think this is what our experience is beginning to show us. Instead of having the collar of restriction loosened around our necks, in a sense it is tightened because we are forced into the position of trying to interpret law, and this is not good practice of medicine.

HIRSCHHORN: It isn't good practice of law either to say that somebody was or was not raped. I think you are doing something that is enormously difficult and is a problem in the court of law. As I understand it you imply that some of these committees simply decided it was not rape.

OVERSTREET: This is true, and as a matter of fact from that has come the suggestion that a decision for therapeutic abortion should be made only if rape is reported at the time of occurrence, either to a policeman or physician, on the grounds that you cannot make the decision later on after the patient missed two periods, as is usually the case.

BURNHILL: You not only become a judicial committee, you become a law enforcer, don't you?

OVERSTREET: This is the bad thing about the forcible rape statute in California—combining a penal function with a medical function. We are not happy about it.

LUCAS: This illustrates a need for a two-way communication system between attorneys and physicians. The mental health provision can't be applied because it is too vague. Then it is unconstitutional because it is too vague and excludes other classes.

OVERSTREET: I am not sure that it points to the need for better communication between attorneys and physicians. I think it points more to the fact that there should be no legal factors in this adjudication, which should be based only upon a doctor-patient relationship.

LUCAS: In order to do this you have to get the law declared unconstitutional.

OVERSTREET: —which we are trying very hard to do.

LUCAS: I don't know whether I would agree with that or not. I don't know of any cases that are going to be brought up any time soon. Based on the testimony you made just now you could get a declaration of the unconstitutionality of the California statute if you would work with the attorneys in California.

OVERSTREET: We have our own cases in San Francisco.

RODRIGUES-LIMA: The Brazilian law penalizes induced abortion severely, but it is true that this law is little, if at all, enforced. Therapeutic abortion is permitted only if a vital indication is at hand, and this excludes, of course, psychological and psychiatric indications. The only vital indication that is legal is a pregnancy resulting from rape. The Brazilian Code of Medical Ethics, in accord with the Brazilian Penal Code, allows therapeutic abortion only if there is no other means to save the life of the patient. This decision can be made only by a committee of three doctors called into conference by the attending physician. To make this decision legal, a written statement must be drawn and signed by the three medical men. One copy remains with the hospital where the abortion will be performed, another copy is filed in the office of the regional Council of Medicine, and a third copy remains in the office of the attending medical man. In emergency cases, the attending physician alone deals with abortion cases, but is required to file a confidential report to his regional Council of Medicine.

Since the penal laws on abortion are practically ignored and little enforced by the authorities, abortions are practiced widely throughout the country. A nationwide survey by my department showed that in 1964, 22.4 per cent of the maternity ward beds were occupied by abortion cases and that 63.4 per cent of these abortions were induced. The care of complicated abortions accounted for 350,000 lying-in days in the Brazilian hospitals.

Three alternatives could correct this situation: (1) enforcement of the existing laws, but this will meet with little success, since so many thousand criminal abortions are performed; only fourteen were prosecuted in one year and no conviction has been forthcoming for lack of legal proof; (2) legalization of voluntary abortions, but this goes against the morals of the people and especially against the belief of the Brazilian leadership and is therefore out of the question; and (3) economic development and a family-planning program. Economic development would be the ideal remedy. Unfortunately, our high population growth rate and our level of national productivity show that economic development will be of small help to control the abortion outburst, especially in the near future. It follows that the only practical way to change the situation with real success lies in a nationwide family-planning program. Such a program was started in 1966 and did achieve encouraging results in increased motivation and changed attitudes. However, since our laws unfortunately mix the concepts of abortion and contraception, some difficulties arise. An amendment of the law is presently being considered in the National Congress in order to make contraception legal. The edicts of Pope Paul, in spite of the overwhelming Catholic population of Brazil, have little, if any, support from the public in this matter of the moral condemnation of artificial birth control methods.

My position concerning induced abortion is the prevailing one in my country, namely, that it should remain an ethical and medical question, based upon medical judgment. The Brazilian code of medical ethics gives doctors ample freedom in matters of such importance.

QUAY: Dr. Overstreet, do you have hospitals which comply with all the specific positive requirements of the hospital licensing statute, and at the same time carry on shyster operations in the hospital?

OVERSTREET: No. The problem we are having is that some of the hospitals that are fully qualified to carry out therapeutic abortions are avoiding doing their geographic share. They are afraid of what the Joint Commission on the Accreditation of Hospitals might say the next time it inspects their hospital and sees that their abortion rate has risen six- to eightfold. There is a hospital in my own city that is doing private therapeutic abortions and sending its welfare cases to the county hospital rather than let its abortion rate go up. This is a much worse problem than any shyster stuff.

WHITRIDGE: Dr. Overstreet, on what grounds might the abortion law be declared unconstitutional?

OVERSTREET: I presume that it would be declared unconstitutional on the grounds that the state has no right to regulate a woman's decision in reproduction. These would be the grounds for unconstitutionality.

WHITRIDGE: And then, we hope, we would have no law.

OVERSTREET: Yes.

WHITRIDGE: I wonder if you aren't running the risk of having a law that would be worse than the present one.

ROEMER: Actually, the cases that would be coming up would be related to the former law, which is the law in almost all the states of the United States. We would hope, through such cases, to establish the general principle of the right of the woman to have an abortion.

QUAY: In the hospital that was organized for profit, profit particularly from abortions, it would be quite possible under the statute as it now reads for the hospital committee to be part of a partnership operating for profit and to record the unanimous opinion and unanimous findings that immediate abortion was absolutely essential in the case, and do this over and over.

OVERSTREET: The safeguard here, of course, is that under the new statute in California, therapeutic abortion can only be performed in a hospital accredited by the Joint Commission. If there were collusion going on it would easily be picked up by the Commission, which would then remove the hospital's accreditation, so that it would then be illegal for that hospital to do therapeutic abortions.

RANDALL: I will present the case for the hospital that does not have a committee and tell you some of the difficulties we have experienced as a result of not having one. In Buffalo there are six hospitals with residency programs. Two of these six are Catholic hospitals and two had chiefs of service who were Catholic although the hospitals were not. (This is a significant factor that was not apparent from the data Dr. Eliot presented to us. There are hospitals, in other words, that are nonsectarian and yet do not permit abortions. This is sometimes due to the influence of specific individuals on their staff.) Of the six hospitals mentioned, only two, then, to all intents and purposes, permit therapeutic abortions. As a result, the rate of interruptions of pregnancy in these two hospitals is quite high.

One of the predictable problems that developed is the fact that the two non-Catholic hospitals that had Catholic chiefs of service did develop committees to rule on abortion (for the staff rules provided for therapeutic abortion), but the committees had the final say, so no therapeutic abortions were done. Some of these cases found their way to the other two non-Catholic hospitals, and the patients were aborted there. This created consternation, as one might imagine, and we had several meetings about this. The suggestion to the two hospitals that were permitting therapeutic abortion was that they should not permit abortions for women who had been turned down by another hospital's committee. Whereupon, at least as a trial balloon, I suggested we have one committee for the six hospitals that would rule on these cases. Of course, this was unacceptable to the other four and didn't get us anywhere.

So we have now reached a point where two hospitals that deliver approximately 30 per cent of the babies do 100 per cent of the therapeutic abortions. One out of every ten private admissions is for therapeutic abortion. On the ward services in these same institutions the incidence of abortion is one in three hundred. I would explain this partly on the basis mentioned earlier, namely that patients come to the ward service at a stage in pregnancy so advanced that abortion cannot be considered. Another factor is that the ward service is conducted by several obstetricians and gynecologists, each taking his turn on service; some of them will not permit therapeutic abortion while they are on service. This raises the question of whether abortion policy should be uniform within a hospital or whether it should vary with each member of the staff. A new problem has developed in the last year, when almost 50 per cent of the patients on our ward service were unmarried and the majority of them were nonwhite. To do therapeutic abortions in this group in any large number would arouse the same objection we are now experiencing in our family-planning clinic, for many of the black population object to these measures in their neighborhoods.

Our policy has been termed permissive by our hospital administration, which is now demanding that we justify our high incidence of abortion. They want to know why we don't at least have a committee. I would like to explain my point of view about this. I feel that if we had a committee the members would be picked either because they believed in permitting abortions or because they would stop the practice of abortion. You could predict what the committee would do. We rest our case with the plea that we want to preserve in our hospital the opportunity for a qualified physician to call in a consultant and do what he and the consultant think is best for a particular patient. This is an individual decision, a confidential matter that doesn't belong in a committee or in a hospital trustee meeting. Whether we will survive with this particular interpretation of the situation or not remains to be seen, but as far as I am concerned, this is the right decision. I personally do not believe, with all due respect to Dr. Guttmacher, that I have ever seen a situation in which a committee seemed to help. We feel that this ought to be left in the hands of each individual member of the staff. If he does not want to do an abortion, then he doesn't have to. If he wants to do so, we don't think someone else should tell him he should not.

HATCHER: I am concerned about the difference in your ratios of one in three hundred for ward patients and one in ten for private patients. This discrepancy has been mentioned by several other doctors for their hospitals. I wonder whether if poor patients are permitted to know that abortions can be obtained in a dignified atmosphere, they won't ask for these abortions just as quickly as private patients. I am concerned as to whether we are really recruiting to make these services available to the poor.

RANDALL: I share your hope that they will avail themselves of these services. At the moment, we believe that few patients in our public services want an abortion. Now, why they don't want an abortion is another problem. Nevertheless, the demand doesn't seem to be there. The public health nurses, the social service workers, the people who are knowledgeable about these families are our hope of reaching these individuals. It isn't the obstetricians that can let them know that this is available, but it is the people who know the families.

BURNHILL: Dr. Guttmacher has proudly referred to the nearly equal ward and private abortion rates at Mount Sinai Hospital. I would like to explain that as residents, we beat the bushes to get cases for that committee so that he could get the ward ratio higher. And we had to beat the bushes not because the patients came to the clinic late, but because the ghetto population of New York got aborted early and didn't have to come to us. Now we have a very large study in Brooklyn that shows that one out of five ward patients admitted to three major obstetrical services are there as a result of induced abortion. The urban ghetto women are getting abortions with total disregard to the consequences.

OVERSTREET: What you are saying in a sense is that the ratio of ward to private patients depends to a considerable degree on the availability of a good criminal abortionist. We have the reverse situation in San Francisco. We have, essentially, no decent criminal abortionist working in San Francisco. As a result, on two comparable services at the Moffet Hospital we are seeing two to four applications for abortion per week. At the county hospital service, which is a service for the indigent, we are seeing five to seven applications a week.

CUSHNER: There is yet another dimension to this question. I was recently asked to see a patient in consultation who was a worker in the Planned Parenthood clinic and was in the hospital with thrombophlebitis. She happened to be the wife of a leader of the militant black power group. Our new abortion law had just become effective and we were addressing ourselves to the problem of how to inform the inner city patient of the availability of this service. The response was, "Forget it." They hate this environment so much that they will come only when they are ill.

OVERSTREET: There is no doubt this is a factor in San Francisco too. Our public contraceptive programs have become much more effective when decentralized from the county hospital into neighborhood family planning areas. There is no question about the existence of that attitude.

HELLMAN: I think we will move on.

LUND: I will try to get back to the original discussion for the evening about the legitimacy of review, and point out how the system works in Rochester, which differs from the system in Buffalo described by Dr. Randall. I dare say that his department has a tissue committee, a perinatal committee, and other committees dealing with the health and welfare of women. We as obstetricians have for twenty-five or fifty years been reviewing and evaluating ourselves and setting up committees for this purpose. I think it would be impossible to get a group of obstetricians to give up the idea that there should be some review for any major procedure affecting maternal welfare. Until there is some great change in our attitudes, then, we are almost bound to have some type of a review committee.

Another point that comes to my mind is that the laws don't really help as much as we think they do. They create a great deal of confusion. With them, you have the responsibility of determining something. How are you going to determine what the patient wants and whether her want is legitimate? The deeper we go into restrictions, rules, and regulations, the more clumsy and difficult this becomes. No so long ago I had a chance to talk with a lawyer about quite another situation and he said that laws follow practice. Perhaps, then, practice should be the standard, and hopefully laws will follow it rather than doing the reverse, which we are doing. When we get down to the nitty-gritty of this business of legality, someone has to initiate the request, and this is the patient. There is no question about that. So, why doesn't she? Is she hampered by environment? By tradition? By fear of the hospital? That we can't say. Is there any reason to believe that a patient will seek therapeutic abortion more frequently than she will seek contraceptives? There is some evidence that she will, because the event is more fully or clearly in her mind. Once she wants it, then, to whom does she turn? Ultimately, she has to turn to a physician, because abortions are done in medical centers by physicians. Here again, I think the physicians can be hampered by an enormous amount of bureaucracy.

In our own institution, any member of our staff can request a therapeutic abortion and would consult with an obstetrician in regard to this. From that point, the matter is referred to the chief of the department concerned and to the chief of obstetrics and gynecology and that is where the buck ends. If this is a psychiatric matter, then the two of us discuss it. If it is a medical matter, the two of us discuss it. I don't know if this is a good system. At least we think it works reasonably well in our setting. There are delays, as there are delays in anything, and this is one of the great criticisms of the committee system.

HELLMAN: And now may we hear from Dr. Cushner?

CUSHNER: I should like to state my views about the means of determining the legitimacy of abortion requests, as a physician from a state with a realistic law which allows abortions to be done by a licensed physician in any accredited hospital as long as it is done for American Law Institute indications and has been approved. It is left to the hospital to decide what mechanism of approval it wants. Problems have already arisen in putting this new law into effect. Four months and eighteen days following the effective date of our new law, we are faced at a community level with non-Catholic obstetricians who refuse to perform this procedure on patients they have cared for through their entire reproductive careers; with hospital trustees who will not revise their by-laws to conform with the new law; with a static indigent abortion rate; and with a deputy Commissioner of Health who requests an audience before the Internal Welfare Committee of our state medical society because of his concern over teen-age births and teen-age pregnancies, wanting to know how our new law can be utilized to solve this problem. The problem of bed utilization has arisen because we are doing the abortions, not for a segment in Baltimore City, but for the entire Eastern seaboard—or so it sometimes seems.

Webster's Dictionary defines legitimacy in two ways: that which is sanctioned by law and custom, and that which is reasonable and logically correct. So the obstetrician has first to determine medical legitimacy—i.e., that which is reasonably and logically correct according to current medical knowledge. From that he evaluates his patients' needs. However, he must also determine legal legitimacy. I share the view of many others that the legal legitimacy of abortion should be identical to the legal legitimacy of any other surgical procedure, that there should be no law that specifies indications or methods of evaluating needs, and that these issues should be governed by the same mechanisms that govern other operative procedures—licensing, hospital staff privileges, hospital staff government, postoperative tissue committee review, and the like.

Since, at this moment, we must consider medical and legal legitimacy, my views are as follows: An abortion should be considered medically legitimate if three facts have been reasonably determined by the physician intending to perform the procedure: (1) there are no discernible factors which contraindicate either the surgical procedure or planned anesthetic or the termination of the pregnancy itself, or both, (2) there is reason to assume that continuation of the pregnancy will put the fetus or the family at risk, and (3) the mother has been informed of the nature of the procedure and desires that it be performed. This is simply applying to induced abortion the same principles which apply to all other surgical procedures.

However, there is one unique feature about induced abortion which does not pertain to any other surgical procedure. The physician, with expertise in performing the surgery, is not necessarily the person with expertise in determining the need. This is obvious and therefore I think consultation should be obtained when, in the opinion of the operating surgeon, he needs it for decision-making. This brings me to two objections which I have to current concepts. One is that a consultation is mandatory in every case. I will call your attention to the abortion indicated because of maternal exposure to a teratogen. The indication for abortion is an increased fetal risk of abnormality due to that exposure. The medical responsibility of the obstetrician is merely to ascertain that the exposure did indeed occur. The abortion is then indicated because of a statistical risk which is known to the obstetrician. My second objection is to the concept that only physicians can be qualified consultants. If abortion is indicated because of emotional disturbances based upon socioeconomic problems or a burden to be imposed by an additional member of an already existing family, I believe that the social service worker or the psychiatric social worker who has perhaps dealt with this family for some time may be a more appropriate consultant than the psychiatrist seeing the mother for one session. Finally, the need for determining legal legitimacy will be called for as long as laws exist. I am not asking the review authority to play lawyer, but neither should it assume the role of judging the judgment of a duly appointed member of that staff. If he is a competent physician and has a hospital appointment, you don't preoperatively review his craniotomies, thoracotomies, or hysterectomies. The role of the abortion review authority, in my opinion, is to ascertain for the hospital that the abortion which is being performed falls within the framework of the law.

QUAY: Is it possible to get any follow-up information about patients who applied for therapeutic abortion but were turned down?

GUTTMACHER: That is a very difficult thing to do. At Mt. Sinai Hospital a man studied fifty patients who had therapeutic abortions on psychiatric grounds, but he had difficulty in finding control cases because many who were refused legal abortions got them done illegally. There have been studies of women who have not had abortions to see how many commit suicide, how many become psychotic. As far as I know there has not been a spectacular amount of trouble. In other words, nothing dramatic happens to women who are refused abortion on psychiatric grounds.

HATCHER: One of the things that concerns me the most is this ratio of three hundred to one versus ten to one. Actually, the social indications are much greater for the poor than for the well-to-do, and twenty-five to thirty years from now those of us who are in the family-planning business may be faced with the strange situation wherein the law tells the poor they have to have sterilization or abortion.

I would like to see a change now—based on a law permitting people to do this voluntarily.

LUCAS: I want to ask Dr. Guttmacher about a statement that he made in his most recent book to the effect that the public in the United

States would not be able to accept a freedom-of-choice plan in which the woman had the right to decide herself. If the courts, in particular the Supreme Court, ultimately decide that a woman has a private right to determine whether she wants to have an abortion, do you think that the medical profession would sabotage this right, through committees and through interposing itself between a woman and her gynecologist?

GUTTMACHER: My statement was based on repeated polls. When you put the question to the American public, Do you favor abortion for anyone who wants it? you do not get more than 20 per cent saying Yes. On the other hand, if you ask, Do you favor abortion for rape or for this or that? it goes up to 85 per cent saying Yes. I would say the American public is not willing to have abortion on demand. They would be willing for themselves, but not for their neighbors. The physician follows the public, he does not lead the public. If 70 per cent of the public says Yes, then we will have abortion on demand. The doctors are not going to lead the public into that attitude, that is all I am trying to say.

HIRSCHHORN: Two contradictory statements have been made and I strongly disagree with both of them. One says that law follows practice and the other one says that practice follows law. They are both wrong. The civil rights law has shown us that practice does not follow law and the outdated 160-year-old sex laws that forbid public kissing have shown that in fact laws do not follow practice. I think one has to accept the fact that right now there are millions of illegal abortions. Unless we do these legally they are going to be done by others, and there is going to be suffering. I think it is as simple as that. Until enough doctors are brave enough to do as Dr. Guttmacher and a number of other people have done, and test these outdated laws which are not being enforced, we are not going to solve the problem. I think we are just pussyfooting around the whole problem.

CUSHNER: Would you endorse some protection for the doctor who has to do it?

Lucas: I would endorse protection for anyone who tests these things for the first couple of years. I don't know what the legal status of a committee would be, for example, in taking the responsibility for an individual's action.

Cushner: What is the ethical and medical position of the physician in an environment where abortion is available on request and the patient walks in requesting abortion and the examination reveals a physical contraindication?

Lucas: Then you are completely within your right as a physician, just as in refusing to prescribe nose drops as somebody said earlier, to deny the abortion.

Cushner: You are changing your statement.

Lucas: No, I am not.

Cushner: Then don't say that you want abortions to be handled by the legitimate doctor in the same way it is handled by the criminal abortionist. He does not evaluate.

Hellman: Yes, he does.

Cushner: You mean the physician abortionist evaluates.

Hellman: Some of our coat-hanger abortionists at least find out how many months pregnant the patient is.

Cushner: I have not run into that.

Randall: One of our real problems is that, as soon as we mention abortion, people think we are talking about sin or murder. Perhaps one of the greatest contributions that somebody could make is a new term that would do for this business what "family planning" has done for birth control. If we could call this something more acceptable than abortion, we would get the public attitude to change a little faster.

ABORTION AND MORALITY

The Relationship between Available Abortion and Sexual Freedom

Garrett Hardin, Ph.D. (moderator)
John V. P. Lassoe, Jr. (rapporteur)
Daniel Callahan, Ph.D.
David M. Feldman, Rabbi
Joseph F. Fletcher, S.T.D.
Wardell B. Pomeroy, Ph.D.
Ralph B. Potter, Jr., Th.D.

HARDIN: By way of setting the stage, I would like to bring up a hypothesis that has been batted around for twenty years in the social sciences. I don't know whether anybody's name is attached to it, but the hypothesis is this: In public affairs, every time you have a change by one order of magnitude, this produces a revolution.

Now, take the example that is most often cited, that of transportation. We used to go at about six miles an hour whether by horse or by foot. That was just about the limit for any extended time. When the automobile came in, we could go sixty miles an hour. This is an increase by a factor of ten, which is called one order of magnitude. And, as you all know, the consequences of this, both economic and moral, have been tremendous.

Think what this has done to the habits of courting—whole new horizons have been opened up in sophisticated courtship because automobiles go sixty miles an hour instead of six.

Now, the question is: Does this rule hold with respect to birth control? I have been thinking about this. A number of people have said that under primitive conditions, probably about eight children was the normal number of children—by "primitive" meaning here perhaps even primeval, before man controlled his birth at all. Eight seems to be about the maximum number, perhaps representing something on the order of sixteen conceptions, with eight children surviving, say, until the age of one. Then, of course, six of those died before they reached breeding age, and you ended up with two, which is just replacement, and so the population remained stable.

We are rapidly approaching the time when the number of live births is going to be very close to two or just slightly above that, and so we have a change from eight to two. That's just about half an order of magnitude, so it doesn't look like it quite fits the definition of a revolution.

However, if you look at it from another point of view—from the point of view of the risk involved—perhaps the risk per individualz active coitus is not the important thing. Christopher Tietze says there's about one chance in twenty-five of pregnancy when the act of intercourse is spaced at random.

Maybe the thing to do is to consider it in terms of a year; in those terms, under primitive conditions, the probability of the woman becoming pregnant before the year was out was, I would say, 0.9 or something of this sort. Maybe 0.95, depending on the amount of sterility, malnutrition, and other factors. It is very close to one. Under conditions of the pill, the probability is about 0.01, as good a figure as any; so there is a decrease in the risk by almost two orders of magnitude. And if we couple with our contraception completely elective abortion, reducing the risk·of unwanted pregnancy as close to zero as we want it, then, of course, this gives you an infinitesimal figure you can't even see.

So I think when we consider contraception coupled with abortion reducing the risk of unwanted pregnancies, this will clearly fill the bill—a change of an order of magnitude of at least one and maybe a good deal more. In this case, the order of magnitude of the risk as perceived by the woman herself, if she has abortion available on request, is zero. And under no other system is this true. This is the revolution that we are facing.

Now, if you go back to the time of the early automobiles, if you think back to the year 1900 when a few of these monsters were putt-putting around, ask yourself: how many people in the year 1900, looking at these dressy little contraptions going around, faced the possible social consequences of this development? It is hard to believe that very many people could have foreseen even a fraction of the social consequences.

And the question is, Can we, with the history of this sort of thing behind us to sensitize us to future possibilities, do any better? Can we foresee the consequences, particularly in moral matters, of this revolutionary change which is at least comparable to the change wrought by the automobile?

Having finished my introductory remarks, I would like to call upon the panelists for their comments. First, Dr. Fletcher.

FLETCHER: I say, as a point for debate perhaps, that abortion is good ordinarily except when medically wrong. But I plan to be careful and, therefore, add: But it could be medically wrong and still be the right thing to do, and it could be medically called for and yet be the wrong thing to do.

I am changing from a position I took a year or so ago in Los Angeles at UCLA where I said that making babies is a good thing, but making love is, too; that we may and should make love, even though no baby is intended; and that there ought to be no unintended and no unwanted babies. And the best way, I said, to make love without babies is to prevent their conception; and the next best way is to prevent fertility itself; and the least desirable way is to end the pregnancy already begun. But any of these methods is good if the good to be gained by their use is great enough to justify the means.

Well, now, I want to change my position. I think, at least potentially, that abortion in the preuterine, prenidation tubal state of the zygote can be quite the best method of fertility control because it would entail, if present research succeeds, the least discomfort and the least risk of failure due to emotion or carelessness and the least hazard of ineffectiveness.

I say, let's be done with all objective morality, that is to say, any notion in terms of scriptural law or natural law, that right and wrong and good and evil are intrinsic values, and take instead the view that all values are quite extrinsic, dependent upon the varieties of circumstances.

It seems to me that we have three possible views if we want to polarize ethical debate about the question of abortion. We can take the view that all abortion is good, or that all abortion is evil, or that it can be good sometimes and not other times; it is the third view that I would push for.

We can force a woman to conceive a child by rape. We can force a woman to bear a child against her will by religious or civil authority (which, by the way, appears to me to be rape at another level). But we cannot force her to want a child and whatever is compelled—I am speaking now as a moralist—whatever is compelled against the will or *contra mentum* is not moral and may be actually immoral—and this is the case in principle for elective abortion, that is to say, abortion upon request, which seems to me to be the soundest possible course.

David Granfield said to us that we cannot sacrifice principle to expediency. I think that the only true morality is precisely expediency, and I hold to Paul's statement in I Corinthians 10: "Even if all things are lawful, they are not all expedient." And this is the basic issue in ethical analysis of all moral problems.

HARDIN: I thought we might hear next from Rabbi Feldman, who has recently completed a book on birth control in Jewish law.

FELDMAN: I want to say that Dr. Jakobovits, who has also written in this field, would have been here together with me, or instead of me, but is not able to. I feel a little bit bad about that because I am going to take such a different position from his and I think that it is unfair that he is not here to hear it.

Dr. Jakobovits has uttered a Jewish point of view with regard to birth control and abortion, and he has taken a very strict stand. He has always been against it, and I think that he has been against it more on social, almost political, grounds (because he just wants more young people born) than on interpretation of strict law as the rabbis have defined it through the generations.

I take the liberty of disagreeing only because I am not saying anything on my own, but rather relying on the decisions of the rabbis through the generations. My book relates all of these cases which, according to the rabbis, are not transferable but are inferable. We can infer from them a lot of very interesting value concepts with regard to the subject.

I am thinking of two rabbis whom I read, one from the seventeenth century and one from the twentieth century. There was a Rabbi Bachrach, who wrote in the eighteenth century in reply to the question of whether a woman who has conceived in adultery could have an abortion. He discussed the entire matter from a legal standpoint, and he said: "Well, as I read Jewish law, there is nothing to prohibit her having an abortion because from the standpoint of the very strict, bare, stark Jewish law, the woman has this right."

Speaking in the context of his very orthodox milieu in Hungary, the nineteenth-century rabbi declared that, even though it is the duty of women to build the world and perpetuate the species, "No woman is required to rebuild the world by destroying herself." And since she doesn't have to destroy herself, then we take her pain, her welfare into consideration.

My other example comes, as I say, from the twentieth century. Rabbi Moshitz Vie, who died in 1965 and was the rabbi at Antwerp, Belgium, discussed the reasons for abortion. After all, a woman can have one if she so decides. We feel that this is important to her well-being, and we interpret well-being to be psychological as well as physical. But she should have good warrant because she is destroying a potential child. And so what is a warrant? And he says: "Well, pain. Pain is an adequate warrant. If she has undue pain, then she certainly is entitled to an abortion."

He quotes something very interesting from another corner of Talmudic law—a civil law, a law that says that if you run over somebody with your car or if your ox gores somebody (before there were cars), then you have to pay fivefold. You have to pay for his hospitalization, you have to pay for his employment that he lost, the wages that he didn't make, and a few other things including embarrassment. You have to pay for the embarrassment. After all, it is embarrassing to get hit by a car or to have your eye blacked or to have your arm in a sling; so this adds to the medical bill and the loss of income. The ones who by negligence caused this have to pay even for your embarrassment, the embarrassment of being sick.

"Well," he says, "here we have precedent that you have to pay for a man's pain as well as for his embarrassment. We know that women are very modest and that a woman is very conscious of her position in society; and if she is going to have the shame—the embarrassment—of giving birth to a child out of wedlock or in wedlock through adulterous relations, well, then, embarrassment is much worse than any physical pain. And certainly if we are going to allow an abortion on grounds of physical discomfort, we ought all the more so to allow it on grounds of social, spiritual, emotional embarrassment—that kind of discomfort."

But he stops short. He says: "If I were to say this, if I were to spell out the consequences of my reasoning, I would open the floodgates to immorality. I would say, 'Well, you know, you go ahead and have premarital sex as well as all the rest because it doesn't matter. Once you have that pain of embarrassment, it is going to be sufficient to warrant abortion.' " So he stopped short because he didn't want to carry the legal reasoning to its social consequences.

I want to go off the subject a little bit and say something about this idea of pain because it is a very interesting one. The Bible says: "Give birth in pain." And, after all, this was the curse of Eve. In 1904, Father Karman in a book called *The Crux of Pastro Amenisis* said that this is tied up with atonement.

Sometimes women feel that they have to go through the pain of an unwed pregnancy in order to atone for their guilt of promiscuity or, better still, for the sin of Eve, which is inherited and has to be expiated, and *is* expiated in terms of the pain and even the danger of a difficult childbirth and so forth. If you have an abortion, you remove those two kinds of expiation for the sin of Eve.

In 1840, when anesthesia was first introduced in the Massachusetts General Hospital, there was opposition by the church to the use of anesthesia. "After all, the Bible says that woman should give birth in pain. Who are we to fly in the face of Providence?" They said to the rabbis: "Look, it is your Old Testament. How do you feel about this?" And the rabbis said: "Well, it's a curse; it is not a commandment. It is not a commandment which is transferable to the descendents of Eve. It is a curse to Eve alone, not to her descendents. To us, we have the commandment of sparing people pain. Anything we can do to spare pain is a commandment; it is a mishna. It is a mishna, therefore, to use the anesthesia to spare pain. It is a mishna to allow woman an abortion if her childbearing or her pregnancy itself cause her undue pain."

Rape is another example. Dr. Jakobovits has again taken a very strict position: if the woman has become pregnant through rape, that fetus is a child like anyone else. Any child has a right to be born, and it is the duty of society to raise this child.

Well, first of all, we don't have any sort of thorough concept like that in Jewish law. The fetus is not yet human. This has been determined in many rabbinic decisions. It may be life, but it is not yet human. It may be a soul. It may go to heaven. It doesn't need baptism. It doesn't need to be brought to a full term, which is another factor very often overlooked in this whole question of ensoulment.

Throughout the Bible and Talmudic literature there is a kind of agricultural metaphor. We speak of the woman as the field, and man plants his seed in the field. The woman nurtures this seed which is implanted within her like the earth does—Mother Earth.

But a rabbi in the nineteenth century, dealing with the question very theoretically in a case that had come before him, said: "Well, yes, she might be like the field, but she is different in that she is human and, being human, she does not have to nurture seed which has been implanted in her against her will. That would militate against her basic humanity. She is not a machine."

This, too, is the kind of pain and discomfort that a woman is just not required to undergo. And certainly in all rabbinic decisions, when it was a matter of the mother versus the child, the mother took precedence because she is alive and human and may ask for pity.

I have many other rabbinic decisions that can be summarized under one very broad generalization. I boil it down to a hypothetical case. If a woman should come before a rabbi and say: "I took thalidomide while I was pregnant," or "I had rubella during pregnancy, and I think the child is going to be deformed, and I want to have an abortion because what kind of a life is that for a child to be born deformed?" the rabbi would probably say No. He would say to her: "How do you know it is going to be deformed? Maybe it is not. And if it is going to be deformed, maybe a life as a cripple is better than no life at all."

But if the same woman should ask the same question from a different standpoint and say: "I took thalidomide," or "I had German measles during pregnancy and the chance that the child is going to be deformed is driving me crazy, is giving me mental anxiety," then the rabbi would say, "By all means, go and have an abortion."

When she speaks about the fetus, she is speaking about something which is not yet born and he can say to her: "Well, the Talmud says you leave the secrets of God to Him. You don't know what is going to be with that fetus." If she speaks in terms of herself—someone alive, standing here today, asking for mercy—then all of the Jewish traditional law and morality which says you concern yourself mainly with the welfare of that woman, all of that is mustered by the rabbis when they say: "Well, go right ahead and have an abortion. We don't want you to have mental anguish."

POMEROY: I find it a bit amusing but also rather frightening to be on a panel which is concerned with morality and abortion. My own background is research in marriage counseling, and I find that I am much more comfortable considering abortion from a physical, psychological, or social standpoint than from a theological or moral viewpoint.

If one considers the fetus to be a human being, then arguments concerning physical, psychological, and social outcomes have very little meaning. If, on the other hand, one does not consider the fetus to be a human being *in utero*, as I do not, then the morality of abortion takes on a totally different meaning.

Others far more knowledgeable than I have grappled with the theological problems of abortion, especially with regard to contraception, where the hierarchy of the Roman Catholic church has taken a peculiarly intransigent position. They have taken the "fetal human being" position, which, in essence, allows for no further dialogue.

It is in the context that abortion is yet another way to control population in the broad sense that I will address my remarks. I feel that perhaps I can offer some resource material, particularly on the question of sexual freedom, but I feel that I don't have much to offer in terms of morality.

I have already co-authored material which has presented data to the effect that the deleterious effects of abortion are, indeed, minor and vastly overshadowed by the positive effects. It has been documented many times that abortions done under proper circumstances by trained physicians are easy, safe, and rarely result in physical complications.

Even after illegal abortions by unskilled abortionists, only 7 per cent of the females reported severe physical difficulties and only 17 per cent reported any physical difficulties beyond the immediate pain. These figures are drawn from our book on pregnancy, birth, and abortion.

Only 3 per cent of the unmarried women who had abortions reported such unfavorable social consequences as gossip, family rejection, loss of friends, dismissal from school, or subsequent trouble in marriage. None of the married women who were sampled reported any social difficulty although I am sure that some does exist—in a limited number of cases.

Although psychological trauma and subsequent psychological impairment as a result of abortion is more difficult to assess, less than 10 per cent in our sample reported regret, psychological upset, or guilt. Other studies have produced varying results, but it appears that the greatest upset, when it does occasionally occur, is shortly after the event and grows less as time goes on.

Clinically, I have observed in my practice in marriage counseling and in psychotherapy that, after an abortion, the majority of women feel relief in freedom from an unwanted pregnancy. For those who do have guilt feelings, this is balanced by realizing that the alternative of having a baby is far worse.

To return to my original point, if one accepts the philosophy that an abortion is the murder of a helpless human being, then one must stop at this point and condemn any sanction of the taking of this life. If one takes the position that the fetus is a potential human being, then one may examine the physical, psychological, and social consequences of abortion. If this is done, I have no doubt that overwhelming evidence will favor sanctioning the practice of abortion.

MOORE: Today's papers and discussions at the conference have been factually enlightening and interesting. Yesterday's emphasis, however, on the issues of ensoulment and nascence, when life begins, and so forth, left me despairing.

This topic is in one sense vitally important. The public controversy surrounding these questions directly influences the legislators. The legislators make the laws, and the laws tell me what I can and what I cannot do. In another sense, however, much of what was said—and I intend no offense toward our distinguished participants—I regard as monumentally irrelevant.

As we indulge in scholarly deliberations here, out there women are having and will go on having abortions regardless of what is concluded here. The comment is sometimes made that when the morning-after pill is perfected, the whole question of whether a fetus is ensouled or not will become academic. I submit that the question already is academic.

The real moral question before us then is whether women shall obtain abortions in the present manner—and one could use such adjectives as degrading, dangerous, humiliating, and expensive—or whether they will have their abortions humanely. If it is immoral to destroy a fetus, the circumstances under which the woman became pregnant would seem to be beside the point. And if it is judged not immoral to do so, these circumstances would still be beside the point.

However emotion-laden and sympathy-provoking such words as "rape," "incest," and "deformity" might be, I have real difficulty understanding those who would haggle over the permissible indications for abortion. The only plausible explanation for this position—a pragmatic, not a logical position—comes from politicians who use what they call the "salami" approach, that is to say a-slice-at-a-time or the-general-public-isn't-ready-for-any-more-yet theory.

The morality issue can only be clouded further by the replication of surveys which ask the public to name the conditions under which they would approve of an abortion. Social scientists are not unaware surely of the effect the questioning has on the people they question. We not only obtain information; we plant notions in our wake and suggest categories of appropriate thought.

Such surveys, dutifully reported by the press, have by now already sufficiently documented the fact that most people of all social categories approve of some liberalization. We found that persons who are white, urban, Northeastern, Jewish, college-educated, and so forth hold the most liberal views on abortion. The surprising findings from Charles Westoff's studies are that women of increasing age levels usually associate with increasing conservatism, but not so in the case of abortion; women who have advanced further in the life cycle are more inclined to take liberal views on abortion. And there are surely very many women who have abortions for social and economic reasons but who, nevertheless, when questioned by an interviewer, would disapprove of these same reasons for abortion for the general public.

I find it hard to take seriously the possibility of increased promiscuity as an argument against abortion. Should we also abolish the automobile? Surely its use has contributed greatly to sexual freedom. Should we introduce a system of chaperonage? For by this method we could assure a greater degree of chastity. A system of morality which relies on fear of pregnancy to bolster it has very little to recommend it.

Moreover, not only is fear of pregnancy not an appropriate deterrent, it cannot even be seen as an effective deterrent. If bringing an unwanted person into the world is a punishment to be meted out to a woman for sexual intercourse, then perhaps we should devise a better, a more immediate, not-delayed-by-nine-months means of punishing her and her alone.

There are some who describe abortion as slaughter of the innocent; maybe they wish that they were talking about nonabortion as punishment of the innocent.

The last issue that I want to raise, truly essential to this problem, has so far been referred to only obliquely at this conference. That is the moral question (not to be disguised as merely a social, psychological, political, or economic question) of whether half the human race is to continue telling the other half what it may and may not do.

One observation we can make is one made so seldom that I am not sure whether it is an observation so obvious that it is not even worth mentioning. It is surely no accident that the primary opposition, although not the only opposition, to abortion reform in this country and in many other parts of the world centers on the leadership, not the membership, but the leadership, of a church which is governed by a celibate male hierarchy. Similarly, countries which have adopted the most liberal policies on abortion, with the exception of Japan, are also not accidentally those countries which recognize most fully the humanity of women and their right to as full control over their lives as men enjoy. In less advanced countries, such as the United States, the pitiful attempts at abortion law liberalization, which insist on hospital review committees, have among other purposes the clear aim of making sure that control of the woman remains in the hands of what are inevitably all-male or nearly all-male committees. The reluctance to relinquish full control to women is not just a matter of response to the Roman church, but must be seen as reluctance on the part of most men of all kinds of religions to divest themselves of one of their prerogatives.

The woman's right at issue is not just a question of who's going to take care of the children if women go to work or a question of whether women can really be as good engineers as men. It is, I urge you all to consider, a truly moral question as well.

CALLAHAN: The relationship between available abortion and sexual freedom can only be clarified by giving the phrase "sexual freedom" greater specification. I want to deal with two possible meanings: sexual freedom as appropriate choice and sexual freedom as sexual safety. The two different meanings overlap to a considerable extent, but I will treat them as distinct here.

Let us then first ask, "What is the relationship between available abortion and appropriate choice?" Putting the question that way, both on a priori and a posteriori grounds, there is much evidence to suggest that available abortion facilitates appropriate choice, particularly if one understands his choice as the choice to have or not to have a child.

The sharp decline in the Japanese birth rate after the Eugenic Protection Law of 1948 relates much more closely to the sharp rise in the abortion rate than to anything else. At both the governmental and private levels, there was a desire for a lower birth rate and smaller families. The permissive abortion law made the realization of this desire possible.

Rumania provides another example. With an apparently widespread desire for smaller families and available abortion to make the realization of that desire possible, the birth rate fell from 24.2 per 1,000 in 1956 to 14.6 per 1,000 in 1965. As with Japan this drop could not be attributed to effective use of contraceptives. Indeed, so dramatic was the decline in birth rate and so alarming to government officials that the law changed in late 1965 in a restricted direction. Since then, reportedly, the birth rate has once again risen.

The evidence available from Czechoslovakia points in a similar direction. There the birth rate has risen and fallen in direct relationship to the stringency with which the law, permissive enough in its working, has been interpreted. There was a steady decline in the birth rate during the early 1960s when the law was loosely interpreted, a rise during 1963 and 1964 when the law was once more strictly interpreted, and a decline after that date when once again the law was loosely interpreted.

In the case of all the countries so far mentioned, there is a discernible and inversely proportional relationship between the legal abortion rate and the birth rate. By contrast, the nonavailability of legal abortion in a country like India or in the Latin American nations correlates with the much slower decline, if any, in the birth rate. Of course, there are a number of variables which must be considered before one draws any general conclusions for the world as a whole.

Let me now define sexual freedom as sexual safety and ask a different question: "What is the relationship between available abortion and sexual safety?" In this instance, one piece of evidence worth looking at is the pronounced decline in the age of women having legal abortions in those countries with abortion available.

In Japan, the percentage of women under 20 having an abortion rose from 1.2 per cent in 1955 to 1.4 per cent in 1964. The percentage of women in the 20–24 age bracket having legal abortions rose from 15.5 per cent in 1955 to 16.5 per cent in 1964. Correspondingly, the percentage of women over 30 having legal abortions dropped from the years 1955 to 1964.

Sweden provides a more pronounced instance of the same trend. The number of women in the 15–19 age group receiving legal abortions rose from 243 in 1960 to 1,080 in 1966; from 328 to 1,300 in the 20–24 age group. Similarly, the number of unmarried women having legal abortions rose from 603 in 1960 to 2,286 in 1966, while the number of legal abortions granted to married women during the same period rose only from 1,644 to 2,773. Since 1965, there has been a sharp rise in the number of abortions granted and in the percentage of applications accepted by the Royal Medical Board, about 92 per cent in 1967. The greatest increase has been in the category of unmarried women under the indication of anticipated weakness.

These figures, of course, represent trends in only these countries. Similar trends can be pointed out in other Eastern European and Scandinavian countries, and they make it reasonable to suppose that the availability of abortion makes it subjectively safer for unmarried women to engage in premarital intercourse, and for younger married women to weather unwanted pregnancies; that is to say, an option is made available to them allowing a nullification of their pregnancies. Sexual safety is thus illustrated by available abortions.

Contraception is the universally acknowledged method of choice both for family limitation and for sexual freedom. Moreover, to make abortion readily available as a means of implementing a desire for sexual freedom, however legitimate this desire, succeeds mainly in obviating speculation about and sensitivity toward the status of nascent human life.

Abortion on demand as a method of achieving sexual freedom whether in terms of appropriate choice or sexual safety suffers from the same moral flaw as the denial of all abortions for the sake of restricting sexual freedom.

Both positions fasten obsessively, rigidly, and narrowly on only one element of what is a complicated moral problem. Abortion and demands for coitus would make the woman's choice the sole determinant of the morality of abortion. Those opposed to abortion would make the purported humanity of fetal life the sole determinant. Neither position in principle requires an analysis of a wide range of evidence and consideration. Single-track moral codes are always dubious and truncated, as much in the problem of abortion as with any other significant moral problem.

POTTER: Abortion is a moral problem in the sense of the congruence between affirmation and performance. In that realm I must confess that I have very great sympathy with those Roman Catholics and other Christians who find that the willingness of an individual to abort is simply incongruent with their profession that they wish to follow the example of Jesus Christ, who gave himself up in self-sacrificial love for others. I do have sympathy with those who see this as a very intense moral dilemma.

My problem is that to take that approach requires certain theological foundations, certain beliefs about the activity of God, about the propriety of Jesus as a model, about the demands of love as sacrifice, which theological beliefs clearly have been eroded and do not exist presently in the minds of most people in our nation. So that while I can sympathize with those who see abortion as very much less than an appropriate pattern of conduct for believers, still I can find no basis for establishing in public law the requirements that one should never abort or that one should abort only on the occasion of a threat to the life of the mother.

So I ought then to say that with regard to the legal question, Should a requirement forbidding abortion be built into the legislation of this country? I intend to say No. But I want to explore the issue.

The word "human" is a powerful word. It has the effect of linking the life of the fetus to our own life, suggesting that there will be a progression in the erosion of the barriers against the taking of life. But the only way you can define "human" in this sense is by asking about the practices of particular groups; there is not a clear-cut biological means of defining the word. This is not a biological question. It is a question of social practice.

I think that what is at stake is the preservation of the very convenient and important principle that human life is to be protected, and the best way of preserving that principle is simply to define certain entities as not being human life which need to be protected. This happens in the case of abortion with those who deny the humanity of the fetus and it happens also in the case of the definition of death of those who are comatose. The way to preserve the principle of protecting human life is to say their life has already ceased, and, therefore, the plugs can be pulled out without jeopardizing this moral requirement of preserving life. In this connection I think that we have neglected to explore the nature and the function of moral discourse and the use of moral terms to find out exactly what they are meant to perform in particular settings.

Let me make one more comment about what I think are the stages of argumentation about legal implementation of laws concerning abortions. There are two stages, it seems to me.

First of all, you have to demonstrate that there are certain harms that flow from allowing abortion or from not allowing abortion. This is an empirical question basically. You can demonstrate that there are harms to the mother as well as to the fetus if that is a point of concern. There might be harms to individual character held to be indispensable for common life. There might be harms to the general ethos, if you are worried about the collapse of fundamental values that make human life decent and possible. Most of our debate is focused on this demonstration of alleged harms or denial of alleged harms.

But a second stage of the argument that has been neglected here, I think, is to show that certain acts must be prevented by the state, that certain people or persons or entities have priority for being granted relief from the harms that they suffer. In other words, in the practice of abortion or in the nonpractice of abortion, there may be harms imposed upon certain subjects.

How do you balance them? Who is to be given preference? Now, the type of argument relevant to that level of dispute is jurisprudential and philosophical in nature, and the full issue cannot be settled by simply adducing the fact that women are indeed injured if the actual subtlety of the debate is that, "Yes, women must bear with their injury now for the sake of the presumed ethos that keeps life in our society together without allowing us to be predatory on one another."

To me, the difficulty is that I can find no adequate grounds, that are not highly speculative, to justify refusing women abortions they strongly desire; so I think that there is no basis in public law for the continuation of existing restraints.

There is a great asymmetrical feature in this debate, for those who want reform can point to vivid harm, to very real people, with whom each of us can identify, and the opponents of reform can speculate upon remote harms to abstract entities with which we cannot identify.

Now, I am powerfully moved by the self-sacrifice shown by those who accept a tragic, unanticipated, unwanted situation. But for those who are not able to find in themselves the basis that makes sense for such behavior, I think you must allow them recourse to abortion.

I think that basically what is happening in the West is the dissolution of the theological foundations that made this type of self-sacrifice meaningful to many. Specifically with conception, it is no longer seen as a providential act of God, by which God calls men and women to assume the vocation of parenthood; but, if conception is not that, if it is not something that comes about by God's specific act, the God who plans and has in mind the welfare of all, if it is simply the result of rotten luck through bungled contraception, then certainly the basis for refusing abortion is eroded in the minds of people, and, as a matter of fact, it is nonsensical not to avail yourself of this privilege.

Since parenthood is a very important matter, it ought to be planned. If God can't be counted upon to plan it, then people should.

HARDIN: I know that many members of the panel would probably like to reply to one another, but I think it is time to throw this open to general discussion. Who would like to speak first? Dr. Guttmacher.

GUTTMACHER: I am a little bit confused, and I think Dr. Fletcher can help me. I believe that he thinks abortion should be purely a matter between the patient and the physician. And what kind of judgment is the physician to make? What are you endowing us with to make the wise decision? We are not religionists. Most of us are not psychiatrists. We are not social workers. We're just plain doctors. And on what basis are we going to say to a woman, "Yes, you should" or "No, you shouldn't have an abortion," if this is going to be a decision between an individual and her physician?

FLETCHER: Professional servants are educated guessers, and many of the problems of human decision-making are more or less problem-atic. Presumably a gynecologist or obstetrician who had no aware-ness of or sensitivity about the social and psychological dimensions of his patients' lives and problems, and focused simply upon the physiology of his patients could not make, in my opinion, a very mature decision with respect to whether to terminate a pregnancy or not.

I would say that abortion should be available to patients if there is no medical contraindication. But, you see, I am quick to add there might be situations you know of in which that generally sound and valid proposition ought not, in fact, to be followed in a given case. And I don't see how it is possible to tie the creative freedom and technical discretion of any professional servant down any more fully than just that. If behind your question, there is some wondering whether we can't establish some prefabricated criteria for when and when not, I would say that you know that's not only probably an unrealizable hope, but potentially quite disastrous.

MOORE: Dr. Guttmacher, I would hope that if the day were to come when this was simply a matter between a woman and her physician that he would neither be in a position to say "Yes, you may" or "No, you may not," nor be in a position to say "Yes, you should" or "No, you should not." He should be there in his role as a physician to tell her about possible medical contraindications.

GUTTMACHER: I was thinking this through when Dr. Fletcher was talking about medical contraindications. There is *no* woman we can't abort, so this idea that a certain proportion of patients cannot be aborted is not a medical concept. So it is not a matter of "Can you?" It is a matter of "Should you?" I don't have difficulty understanding the "can," but I have difficulty understanding the "should."

MOORE: I would hope that it never would be interpreted that it was the physician's role to say, after the consultation, "Yes, I think you should," or "No, I think you shouldn't." I would hope that he would view his role as helping the woman to see what the alternatives are, medically and socially, to make sure that an abortion is what she really wants.

HARDIN: I have a feeling we have a conflict between sovereignties. Miss Moore is asserting the sovereignty of a woman to get what she wants, and aren't you, Dr. Guttmacher, asserting the sovereignty of physicians to refuse to perform their offices?

MOORE: Refusing responsibility is all that you men are saying. This is a decision to be made between the patient and the doctor.

GUTTMACHER: Then, if a woman says that she wants to be aborted and we can't persuade her from this course, then we simply act as a rubber stamp and do it. That's a simple problem.

HARDIN: Then my question is: Would you be willing to accept the role of rubber stamp or do you rebel at that?

GUTTMACHER: I would be unhappy.

HARDIN: Yes, you would be unhappy, and this may be a significant thing. And how can we keep the doctors happy and give the women what they want?

R. HALL: We are talking about two ends of a spectrum really. At one end, people have said that there must be medical indications for abortion, and now we are talking about medical contraindications. There are virtually no medical indications for abortion and there are virtually no medical contraindications against abortion. So, really, you can forget those two extremes and focus on all the areas between them.

I would place the doctor in the role of a technician, simply wielding the curette, but not solely at the insistence of the patient. She should receive some guidance, not necessarily from a doctor, but perhaps from some agency such as the Mothers' Aid Centers they have in Denmark. Through such an agency she could be led to explore the alternatives to abortion—such as getting married and having the child. Then if she still wants the abortion she should have it. When it comes to the doctor, I think he is eventually going to be no more than a technician. This may be humiliating to him. But it is his unavoidable plight if we are to grant women their inherent right to abortion.

SCHUR: I wonder whether Miss Moore then would approve a policy under which doctors would be compelled to abort those who had thought through their problems and decided they should have an abortion—but where the doctor considers, on conscientious grounds, that such an abortion would be inadvisable. It seems to me this potentially and theoretically could be the situation into which we would be pushed if this were carried to extremes.

MOORE: I feel that it is difficult to compel anyone to do something that is against his conscience. It is just as wrong to compel the physician to perform an abortion if he feels it is against his moral feelings as it is to compel the woman to complete the pregnancy.

I don't know what you would do in a town where the physicians all felt that way. I hope the woman would be assisted by some societally arranged structure to find what she needed somewhere else. Our towns aren't that far apart. I think that the issue that was raised this morning about federal funds—public funds provided for such hospitals—should be seriously rethought.

BAUMGARTNER: We are skirting a problem which we have avoided all through this conference, because we are acting as if all we have to do is change a law. This is hocus-pocus, for it assumes that the service that people need is going to be made available overnight. None of this is true. We can change the law overnight, but with medical care services as we have them in this country, abortion will not be available to everybody.

FISHER: I would like to remind Dr. Guttmacher of what we said in the Governor's Commission in New York State where, I think, we felt that after the woman had done a great deal of soul-searching and decided that this is what she wanted, that before it be committed, we would tell her to take some type of spiritual guidance first, rather than just leave it up to her and the doctor. Do you remember that, Dr. Guttmacher?

GUTTMACHER: Yes, but you know that was done because the majority of the commission was in favor of it. But it doesn't mean that each of us was in favor of it. For instance, there are a lot of people that are agnostics, and to make an agnostic go to a rabbi or priest to consult on abortion would be, I think, ridiculous.

LAIDLAW: I would like to take this discussion off on another tack. I was very impressed with the way Miss Moore cut through a lot of brambles in our total discussion of this conference and came down to the practicalities and realities of the situation—the woman who needs an abortion. And it made me wonder whether this discussion does not represent a holdover in our thinking about the Judeo-Christian attitude toward sex per se.

The prime leaders in religion in past times—and to a large degree up to the present—were those dedicated to a life of chastity. We have the statement from St. Paul that it is better to marry than to burn, giving the idea that the sexual life is something in a secondary category; and I wonder whether now we should not, with a greater understanding of what man's sexuality in general, and medicine and psychiatry in particular, have given us, come to the point of saying in loud, resounding tones, *"Sex is good,"* and build a morality on that basis. This is a very important type of experience that begins in early years and carries on through the period that we used to call the innocence of childhood, which is far from being without sexual experience, as we well know.

In looking at the matter of abortion, some of the past arguments have been made in the sense that if you leave abortion as something that is hard or impossible to get, it will in some way suppress this bad thing, this sexuality of man that we want to keep curbed, rather than to help it be developed in a way that society has not developed it at any time, namely, in accord with the total health and normality of the individual.

POMEROY: I have three pieces of data that bear tangentially on what Dr. Laidlaw said. We tried to assess the effect of premarital abortion on marriage and particularly on sex in marriage. First, in our sample of 7,000 women, we took all of those between the ages of 31 and 35; by this time, most of them who were going to get married were married. We found that 62 per cent were married among those who had premarital intercourse. Of those women who had had premarital intercourse, 73 per cent married after the premarital intercourse. If they had had premarital intercourse and gotten pregnant, 74 per cent were married. And our conclusion was that the wages of sin were marriage.

A second statistic. We took all the women who had a premarital abortion and subsequently married and compared them with the women who had had a premarital intercourse but had not had a premarital abortion, to see what sort of a sexual adjustment these two groups of women made during the first year of marriage, and we found no difference in terms of their capacity to have orgasm in the first year of marriage.

And lastly, we tried to ascertain what happened to the divorce rate or the break-up rate of the marriage between those girls who had a premarital abortion and those who had not, and again we found no difference.

FELDMAN: I want to respond to several points. First of all, I'd like to say that I think the Jewish and Christian traditions have many similarities. The one point in which they are diametrically opposed is this attitude toward sex. Sex is not even intrinsic to Christianity. There is an obvious antisexual bias within the Christian tradition.

On the other hand, I think there is a second strain in the Christian tradition. It is an antiheathenistic idea. In other words, pleasures are good, but we don't want to devote ourselves to pleasures. And sometimes celibacy and sacrifice, devotion and consecration to God, is better than this kind of pleasure. So the commonly believed antisexual bias is somewhat mitigated.

But I must say that in Judaism there is no such thing as an antisexual bias, although there is a bias against illicit sex, to be sure. Sex within marriage is to be emphasized, it is to be celebrated, it is to be glorified. Homosexuality and masturbation and adultery and incest—all of these things are illicit sex, and that is what the rabbis worried about. They wanted to keep sex within marriage. Once it is in marriage, there is no element of antisexual bias within Judaism.

LAIDLAW: This is such a big subject that we can only take a small bite. But as a practicing psychiatrist (and I think most of my colleagues will agree with me) I would say that there is nothing that requires more man-hours of work with patients than trying to repair and bring into realistic focus the misinformation and the guilt which patient after patient after patient recounts with regard to masturbation, while we know through Kinsey's studies that it is practically a universal phenomenon in the male and a 60 to 70 per cent phenomenon in the female.

To have a Christian ethic or a Jewish ethic or what have you branding masturbation as something which is depraved and to be regarded as sinful is so entirely against the facts of the case that I can have no patience with it. The psychiatrist has to be a repairman spending hours and hours of his time in trying to remedy the psychoneurotic casualties that come from this basic teaching which is contrary to life itself.

FELDMAN: I want to bring this back to abortion and say that this is not behind our particular attitude against abortion; that is, that because sex is bad, therefore, it should be punished. On the contrary, sex in marriage is good; the illegitimate kind is bad. From the standpoint of the Jewish tradition, abortion is not immoral; it is completely permissible on demand, so to speak, except that the rabbis try to safeguard potential life.

D. HALL: In two years, half of the people in this country will be twenty-five or under. Somehow we are going to have to provide them with basic information and basic service, for they are going to get it some way or another. We heard testimony to this today when Dr. Gold said that a hippie came to a free clinic and said, "If you don't give me an abortion, somebody else will." The same thing is true in the free clinic where I work part of the time. This is the attitude not of just a little group of people, but of half the people in this country.

Furthermore, I don't see this as a question of whether to keep a fetus alive, but rather a question of what we can do about the quality of the people who are right here now. When you work in social agencies for a few years and are exposed to all of the problems of unwantedness, of little babies that are being beaten to death, dropped on their heads, and so on, then it no longer seems to be a matter of keeping some blob alive because it may potentially grow into an unwanted child. I'm sorry, I don't see it that way at all.

CALLAHAN: I do not agree with the traditional Roman Catholic position. I have said that I am in favor of abortion on request. My plea is for the value of detailed intellectual discussion of points. I absolutely agree with what has been said about points. I was disagreeing with the idea that these technical, subtle discussions are not worthwhile discussions.

BAUMGARTNER: Will they help things? The question I want to ask is this: Do you feel that the kind of discussions that you are defending are necessary in order to change the point of view of the establishment?

CALLAHAN: Here is the way I argue against my conservative Roman Catholic brethren. I say precisely that there is far more to the question of abortion than the question of fetal life. There is the problem of the battered child. Let's get this into the equation. There is the problem of the terribly depressed woman. There is the problem of her wishes. And I find that I can be fairly persuasive when I argue with them about this.

But, at the same time, when I am in a group like this, I want to say: "Well, look. I am willing to try to make the issue more subtle for them; could you perhaps tolerate some subtlety on ensoulment and say these issues *are* relevant?"

D. HALL: But if that sort of debate continues, then the state legislatures will hide behind that kind of argument, and anybody else who has any qualms at all will hide behind that kind of argument. Yet a good many who see the problem as imminent want something done as soon as possible. And to continue and perpetuate the kind of discussion that has gone on—

CALLAHAN: I'll accept that if you will privately concede that these are not totally stupid things to be considered.

MARGOLIES: I feel that all of our structural law in the Western world is predicated on the notion of sacredness of life, and it is necessary, I think absolutely indispensable, that we take up the question of when this glob, this protoplasm as a whole that we are discussing, actually begins to assume humanity to the point where we can consider it a human being and, therefore, whether we would be guilty of killing something that's really human, not just potentially human, or whether we are just eliminating something that stands in the way of the happiness and the security of a mother. So I think that this discussion has a place.

I was somewhat taken aback at the sentimental suggestion that we get back to the old Christian concepts of accepting suffering as part of our way of life, accepting the model of the life of Jesus as something for us to emulate and, therefore, accepting suffering as a sacrifice; and that perhaps a mother should accept the burden of bringing a child into the world as a form of emulating that discipline of sacrifice. I think that this kind of nostalgia can be exaggerated to a very great extent, particularly in a suffering world.

I think that our impatience with things as they are and our desire to create a more ideal kind of society and a more ideal, happier situation for women is a part of a better striving. And I think that this yearning for the life of sacrifice and expiation is the reverse of the sort of progress that we are trying to achieve.

POTTER: I think that you have to strive. I think it is important to do so. I am surely not making the claim that suffering is good. I am making the claim that, in striving to overcome injustice, one may have to take a considerable amount of abuse and inconvenience and sacrifice, if you will, in contending for your neighbor's good. And that is something that I find admirable.

So I would find it within myself to counsel someone so minded that that sacrifice is worthy, but I am by no means saying that they ought to accept what is for them meaningless sacrifice or that the state ought to require it from those who aren't so disposed. I think that there is something to be said for the contribution made for our common life by people who accept a badly deformed child and raise it and find this to be a model that has meaning for all of us.

MOORE: I just want to set the record straight. I have obviously given the wrong impression to those of you who think that I have said that we should have no time for the ethical or moral discussions in this conference. I didn't mean to imply that. I feel, of course, that these subjects have a place in this conference but that there are other issues that we should have considered as well.

KNUTSON: We all seem to have a high regard of the individual for his uniqueness, for his freedom of choice, for his human dignity, for his right to justice, and for his right to make decisions for himself. And we have this range of thought about when a human life begins, when a life begins, if it is human or not, and what factors make it human. But we also have feelings about the right decisions for human justice and human rights. It is my feeling that we cannot impose our decisions on others any more than we can let them impose theirs on us.

These are very important issues. We have to find a way to solve the dilemma. And we won't do it if we decide for others as a group, no matter how we decide, when life begins, when a fetus becomes a full-valued human, who has the right of control over it, who has the right of saying whether it should or should not be aborted, or anything else. This means that, in order to communicate some of our own ethical positions regarding some of these basic quarrels to others, we have to provide them with the same freedom of choice that we demand for ourselves.

ABORTION AND MORTALITY

The Medical Risks
Inherent in Abortions Aseptically Performed

Peter Diggory, M.B., B.S., B.Sc., F.R.C.S., M.R.C.O.G. (moderator)
Christopher Tietze, M.D. (rapporteur)
Antonin Cernoch, M.D.
Gunnar af Geijerstam, M.D.
Sung-bong Hong, M.D., M.P.H.
Minoru Muramatsu, M.D., Dr.P.H.
Franc Novak, M.D.

DIGGORY: We are going to discuss both mortality and morbidity of therapeutic abortion. There are quite a number of factors we should look into, affecting mortality and morbidity, such as the period of gestation at which we carry out a termination and the type of operation which is done.

In reference to morbidity, we want to hear about both the immediate effects and the late effects, such as secondary infertility, as related to period of gestation and type of abortion.

I would like to start by giving you some statistics for the United Kingdom. From 1962 through 1966 we had 19,620 therapeutic abortions in the National Health Service hospitals of England and Wales and perhaps 73,000 in private practice, altogether about 93,000. During this period, 22 deaths associated with therapeutic abortion were reported, corresponding to a mortality rate of 24 per 100,000 abortions. During the first 5 months under the new law, 13,042 therapeutic abortions were reported, with 2 deaths. We have no statistics on morbidity.

I am going to ask Dr. Tietze to give us a short summary of his computations relating to mortality due to abortion and to certain types of contraception.

TIETZE: I should like to present a statistical model designed to illustrate the relationships between mortality associated with the reproductive process under various assumptions as to contraception and abortion (Table 1).

Table 1 Illustrative Annual Rates of Pregnancies and of Deaths
Associated with Contraception, Pregnancy, and Abortion
per 100,000 Sexually Active Women of Reproductive Age

	Pregnancies	*Deaths**
A. No contraception, no abortion	50,000	10
B. No contraception, all pregnancies aborted out of hospital	100,000	50
C. Ditto, in hospital	100,000	3
D. Highly effective contraception	insig.	3
E. Moderately effective contraception, no abortion	10,000	2
F. Ditto, all pregnancies aborted out of hospital	10,000	5
G. Ditto, in hospital	10,000	0.3

Assumed mortality rates:

  20 per 100,000 pregnancies (excl. abortion)
  50 per 100,000 abortions out of hospital
   3 per 100,000 abortions in hospital
   3 per year per 100,000 women using highly effective contraception

The model is concerned with 100,000 sexually active women,
married or otherwise, of reproductive age, exposed to the risk of
pregnancy. The following rates of mortality are assumed for this
population:

1. Maternal mortality from complications of pregnancy and
childbirth, excluding abortion: 20 deaths per 100,000 pregnancies.
This corresponds to the level of maternal mortality of the white
population of the United States.

2. Mortality associated with illegal abortion out of hospital: 50
deaths per 100,000 abortions, a very rough estimate, based on an
educated guess of 1,000,000 abortions and 500 deaths per year in
the United States.

3. Mortality associated with legal abortion performed in hospitals, at an early stage of gestation: 3 per 100,000, based on current
statistics from Eastern Europe.

4. Excess mortality from thromboembolic disease associated with
the use of oral contraceptives: 3 deaths per 100,000 users per year,
based on the studies recently published in Great Britain.

Line A of Table 1 shows 100,000 women using no contraception
and having no induced abortions. Assuming a modicum of breast-

feeding, conception would occur at intervals of about two years, resulting in 50,000 pregnancies per 100,000 and 10 deaths associated with these pregnancies.

Line B assumes no contraception, but all pregnancies are aborted out of hospital. Because gestation and the postgestational anovulatory period are substantially shorter than under the assumption of Line A, the number of pregnancies rises to 100,000, with 50 deaths.

In Line C the abortions are performed legally in hospitals, with 3 deaths instead of 50.

Line D assumes a highly effective type of contraception practiced by all women, such as oral contraception under the combined regimen. The number of pregnancies is insignificant; the number of deaths equals that shown on the preceding line.

Lines E, F, and G all assume a less effective but completely safe type of contraception, permitting 10,000 unintended pregnancies. In Line E there is no induced abortion and, therefore, 2 deaths. Line F assumes that all pregnancies are aborted out of hospital, with 5 resulting deaths. In Line G the abortions are performed in hospital and the number of deaths among the 100,000 women drops to 0.3 per annum.

It is obvious that the number of deaths in each line depends on the level of mortality selected, and I certainly would not claim that the differences between Lines C, D, E, and F are in any way significant. Line G tells another story, having a level of mortality lower by a factor of 10.

The following is my conclusion, based on this model: in terms of the associated risk to life, the most rational way of regulating fertility is to use a perfectly safe, although not necessarily 100 per cent effective, method of contraception and to terminate pregnancies resulting from contraceptive failure under the best possible circumstances, i.e. in a hospital operating room.

I have no comparable data on morbidity, but I suspect that the relationships would be similar to those demonstrated for mortality.

DIGGORY: I am sure you will all agree that this is an interesting speculation as to the safest way in which we might handle our population problem.

I think we will go straight from Dr. Tietze to Dr. Muramatsu, and ask him about the situation in Japan.

MURAMATSU: It is very difficult to arrive at accurate statistics on mortality or morbidity associated with induced abortion. This is true even if the abortions are performed legally by physicians.

The largest survey of such abortions, involving 108,055 cases, was conducted in Japan in 1954 by the organization of what we call the "designated physicians." This term refers to those doctors who have been authorized by the local medical organization to perform induced abortions. The suspicion is justified that they may have been reluctant to report all harmful side effects and even all deaths associated with the abortions they had performed. As you can see in Table 2, 3.8 per cent of the women undergoing legal abortion suffered harmful effects. The rate was slightly lower for the large majority of women aborted within the first three lunar months of gestation. It is worth noting that the incidence of harmful effects is greatest for abortions during the fourth month of gestation. This may be due to the fact that some of the designated physicians tended to use D and C at a stage of pregnancy when other methods would have been more appropriate.

Table 3 shows the distribution of harmful effects by type. The total number (4,334) is larger than the number of women with side effects in the preceding table (4,140). This discrepancy is due to the fact that for some women more than one harmful effect was

Table 2 Immediate Harmful Effects Associated with Induced Abortion, by Month of Pregnancy: Japan, 1954

Month of Pregnancy	Number of Induced Abortions Reported	Number of Cases with Harmful Effects	Harmful Effects per 100 Abortions
Within first three months	92,538	3,325	3.6
Fourth month	3,398	282	8.3
Fifth month	3,240	210	6.5
Sixth month	2,343	130	5.5
Seventh month	853	47	5.5
Month unknown	5,683	146	2.6
Total	108,055	4,140	3.8

Table 3 Kinds of Immediate Harmful Effects Associated
with Induced Abortion: Japan, 1954

	Frequency		*Per Cent*
1. Bleeding	3,279		75.7
a) Excessive bleeding at the time of induced abortion		779	
b) Protracted bleeding after the operation		2,500	
2. Infection	1,033		23.8
a) Inflammation of the uterus (cervical catarrh, endometritis, myometritis)		702	
b) Adnexitis		242	
c) Pelvic peritonitis, parametritis		82	
d) Peritonitis		7	
3. Others	14		0.3
a) Temporary weakness of the heart		8	
b) Others		6	
4. Deaths	8		0.2
Total	4,334		100.0

reported. About three out of four cases involved either excessive
bleeding at the time of induced abortion or protracted bleeding after
the operation. Most of the remaining fourth involved some type of
inflammation of the pelvic organs, ranging from endometritis to
pelvic and abdominal peritonitis. A total of eight deaths was
reported in this series, corresponding to a mortality of 7.4 per
100,000 cases. It is worth noting that the data were collected
approximately 15 years ago.

In 1963 the Family Planning Federation of Japan initiated a
series of studies designed to evaluate the immediate and long-term
effects of induced abortion on the woman's health and on her future
pregnancies. The results of these studies, published in 1966, can be
summarized as follows: Menstruation is slightly delayed for two or
three months immediately after the abortion, but soon reverts to the
pattern established before the pregnancy. The investigators reported
an increased incidence of spontaneous abortions and premature
birth, but could not establish a statistically significant association
between a history of induced abortion and either ectopic pregnancy
or secondary sterility. The course of delivery was unaffected. Psychological sequelae were not included in the investigation.

DIGGORY: Our next speaker is Dr. Novak from Yugoslavia.

NOVAK: I do not have satisfactory statistics on abortions for all of Yugoslavia, but I can give you some data on the Republic of Slovenia, which has a population of approximately one and three-fourths million. During the eight years from 1961 through 1967 a total of 70,000 legal abortions were performed. In addition, 35,000 other women were admitted to hospitals with incomplete abortions. According to my estimate, one-fifth of these cases may have been criminal abortions. The number of births was approximately 210,-000.

Among the 70,000 legal abortions there were 4 deaths, corresponding to a mortality rate of 5.7 per 100,000 abortions. The number of deaths associated with incomplete abortion was 47, but it should be noted that some of these women were admitted from outside Slovenia for treatment with an artificial kidney which is available at our University Hospital.

DIGGORY: Would you say a few words about your observations on Rh-sensitization?

NOVAK: Over the past ten years, 656 samples of blood of Rh-sensitized women were seen at the Institute for Blood Transfusion in Ljubljana. Among these 656 women, 51 were nulliparous and had been sensitized by abortion, either spontaneous or induced. Among these 51 women, 18 had experienced abortion in the third, fourth, or fifth month of pregnancy. The remaining 23 women had aborted earlier. Our colleagues in Zagreb, Croatia, have observed a rapid increase in the number of Rh-sensitized primiparae since 1966, following increasing use of the suction currettage. This matter certainly deserves intensive study.

Hrubisko and his co-workers in Czechoslovakia stated in 1964 that Rh-sensitization during the early months of pregnancy is not possible because Rh antigens are not yet present in the red blood cells of the fetus. However, in 1967 a Swedish author, Bergström, demonstrated the presence of Rh antigen in the erythrocytes of a fetus 10 mm in length.

DIGGORY: I would now ask Professor Hong to give us his figures from Seoul.

HONG: Vital statistics in Korea are far from complete or accurate; according to the best available estimate not more than one-half of all births and deaths are registered. We have tried to estimate the number of deaths resulting from induced abortion in Seoul. For this purpose we have used two different approaches. Firstly, we have reviewed all records of women of reproductive age who died in the 11 principal hospitals of the city in 1967. This search produced 18 cases of postabortal infection and 4 cases of postabortal hemorrhage. The second approach involved 690 interviews with survivors of women whose deaths were registered in 1967. This procedure yielded 27 deaths following abortion. Taking into account what is known about the completeness of death registration and of the admission practices of the various hospitals, it is our best estimate that the number of deaths following abortion in Seoul was somewhere between 30 and 50. Since the number of induced abortions in the city appears to be somewhere between 40,000 and 50,000 per year, the estimated mortality rate is between 60 and 125 per 100,000 abortions.

In reference to morbidity, I would like to present a few figures from a study of abortion conducted in Seoul in 1964. These data are based on interviews with about 3,200 women who reported almost 1,500 induced abortions among a total of 12,400 pregnancies. As you can see in Table 4, 36 per cent of these abortions were associated with some physical complaint while no complaint was voiced in 64 per cent of the cases. The incidence of complaints tended to increase with the duration of pregnancy. The lower panel shows that the overwhelming majority of induced abortions in Seoul had been performed by specialists in obstetrics and gynecology and that the incidence of complaints was higher in those cases that had been handled by general practitioners and by nonmedical personnel. About one-fifth of the complaints were described as "very severe," another one-fifth as "severe," and the remaining three-fifths as "not so severe." Of the women who had complaints, 88 per cent recovered within one week, including 77 per cent of those with very severe complaints, 82 per cent of those with severe complaints, and

Table 4 Per Cent Distribution of Induced Abortions by
Presence or Absence of Complaints: Seoul, 1966

	Total		Complaints	
Specified Characteristics	*Number*	*%*	*None*	*Some*
Total	1,484	100	64%	36%
1. Duration of pregnancy at time of abortion				
1 month	496	100	65	35
2 months	649	100	66	34
3 months	254	100	61	39
4 or more months	85	100	51	49
2. Agent performing abortion				
Specialist	1,374	100	65	35
General practitioner	66	100	56	44
Other	44	100	52	48

95 per cent of those with not so severe complaints. Recuperation was
delayed when the pregnancy had advanced beyond the third month.

DIGGORY: Our next speaker is Professor Cernoch from Prague.

CERNOCH: I shall report on mortality associated with legal termination
of pregnancy in Czechoslovakia. During the period 1958–1967
approximately 830,000 legal abortions were performed in our
country. A total of 23 deaths during or following these operations
was reported, corresponding to a mortality rate of 3 per 100,000
legal abortions. A postmortem was performed in each case. I am a
member of the committee concerned with the evaluation of these
deaths and have seen all the documents concerned.

During the same period from 1958 to 1967, approximately
265,000 cases of so-called spontaneous abortion were admitted to
hospitals. How many of these abortions are actually criminally
induced we do not know. During the past six years, only 500 cases
were prosecuted.

Among the fatal cases of legal termination of pregnancy, medical
indications predominate over social indications, although among all
legal abortions, medical indications represent only 13 per cent. The
following is a list of the causes of death.

Thromboembolism of the pulmonary artery	4
Cerebral thromboembolism	2
Air embolism	3
Anesthesia deaths	3
Septic complications	6
Intestinal obstruction	1
Uremia	2
Thecoma	1
Leukemia	1

In most cases the death was caused by neglect of basic medical rules and official instructions for the performance of legal abortion.

Four cases of sepsis were associated with the use of laminaria or bougies and two of the three cases of air embolism occurred during the introduction or removal of laminaria. As a result, the use of laminaria or bougies for the termination of pregnancy has been prohibited by the medical authorities of Czechoslovakia. The third case of air embolism, involving two liters of air, occurred during a vacuum curettage, caused by a reverse connection of tubing, which resulted in blowing air into the uterus.

One case of uremia followed the intraovular injection of 300 ml of 10 per cent sodium chloride solution in a patient with nephrosclerosis and hypertonia. In the second case the patient was aborted when any kind of operation was contraindicated by the uremia. Thromboembolism tended to occur among older multiparous women with either varicose veins or thrombophlebitis of the lower extremities or both. This complication occurred from the third to seventh day after the abortion. Apparently little attention was paid to the presence of contraindications. We recommend not operating on patients with varicose veins until after successful treatment. After the abortion, careful attention must be paid to postoperative treatment for a protracted period of time.

Cerebral embolism occurred in women with endocarditis or ischemic heart disease. This risk is greatest in older women. During the early years deaths tended to be associated with the termination of pregnancies further advanced than 12 weeks and with simultaneous sterilization. Since 1962, termination of pregnancy after 12 weeks of gestation has been permitted only for serious medical indications and it is thought to be inadvisable to perform tubal ligations immediately after curettage. The former operation should be done a few days later, and only in cases without inflammatory complications. It is further recommended that vaginal hysterotomy be done in cases of advanced pregnancy. A careful examination of the heart and kidneys is important, especially in older women.

DIGGORY: I shall now ask Dr. Tietze to read for us a communication by Professor Imre Hirschler in Budapest, entitled "Morbidity and Mortality from Abortion in Hungary, 1960–1967." It had been our hope that Professor Hirschler would be with us at this conference, and he expected to attend, but a couple of weeks ago he let us know that he would not be able to come.

TIETZE: I am very happy to act as a mouthpiece for Dr. Hirschler.

The data in this report were obtained from the Department of Statistics of the Hungarian Ministry of Health.

The number of spontaneous hospital abortions (33,000 to 35,000, as shown in Table 5) requires some explanation, since it is consistently double the number (16,000 to 18,000) one would expect from the percentage (10 to 12 per cent) of pregnancies commonly found to terminate in miscarriage. It is thought that the following explanations account for this higher-than-to-be-expected incidence:

1. Since a small hospital fee is charged for induced abortions done for nonmedical reasons, gynecologists sometimes circumvent this requirement by admitting patients to the hospital on the pretext of spontaneous bleeding.

2. Since induced abortions must by law be performed at the hospital in the patient's area of residence, doctors who wish to accommodate women from outside this area must, again, admit them on the pretext of bleeding.

3. Since some women, due to fear, ignorance, or disdain of requesting a legal abortion, still resort to criminal abortion and since they are admitted to the hospital if complications arise, these cases are also registered as spontaneous abortions.

Mortality associated with legal abortions has been minimal (see Table 6).

Altogether, between 1960 and 1967, there were 31 deaths associ-

Table 5 Obstetrical Events in Hungary, 1960–1967

	1960	1961	1962	1963	1964	1965	1966	1967
Number of live births	146,461	140,365	130,053	132,335	132,141	133,009	138,489	148,886
Number of live births per 1,000 population	14.7	14.0	12.9	13.1	13.1	13.1	13.6	14.6
Number of legal abortions (in 1,000s)	162.2	170.0	163.7	173.8	184.4	180.3	186.8	187.5
Number of "spontaneous abortions" (in 1,000s)	33.8	33.7	33.9	34.1	34.3	33.7	33.6	34.9
Number of all abortions (in 1,000s)	196.0	203.7	197.6	207.9	218.7	214.0	220.4	222.4
Legal abortions per 1,000 15–49 year old females	65.2	68.6	66.1	70.1	74.3	71.6	73.0	72.1
Legal abortions per 100 live births	111	121	126	131	140	136	135	126

Table 6 Deaths Associated with Legal Abortions: Hungary, 1960–1967

Cause of Death	1960	1961	1962	1963	1964	1965	1966	1967
Hemorrhage	–	–	–	–	–	–	–	–
Sepsis and peritonitis	–	–	3	1	1	–	–	–
Other	6	3	5	3	1	2	3	–
Perforation of the uterus	1	–	–	–	–	1	1	–
Total	7	3	8	4	2	3	4	0

ated with 1,408,700 such abortions or 2 per 100,000. During the same period, there were 173 deaths associated with 272,000 so-called spontaneous abortions or 64 per 100,000. Over the years this rate has tended to decline, perhaps due to a decrease in the number of criminal abortions.

The legalization of abortion in Hungary has resulted in a significant reduction in the overall mortality due to abortion.

Early morbidity associated with legal abortions is shown in Table 7. The rate of late complications is more difficult to determine. The incidence of spontaneous abortion, ectopic pregnancy, placenta previa, placenta accreta, and uterine atony has not increased since the legalization of abortion. The incidence of prematurity has increased, but this may be attributed at least in part to greater urbanization, an increase in the number of working women, and the greater prevalence of smoking. However, there is evidence suggesting

Table 7 Complications per 1,000 Abortions: Hungary, 1960–1967

	1960	1961	1962	1963	1964	1965	1966	1967
Perforation of the uterus	1.41	1.46	1.27	1.21	1.23	1.12	0.82	0.93
Fever of gynecological origin	5.72	4.98	4.88	3.52	3.75	3.81	3.78	4.81
Hemorrhage after the abortion	6.27	6.84	6.94	5.17	6.19	6.61	6.19	7.27
Readmission within 4 weeks for fever due to the abortion	5.29	5.26	5.11	4.43	4.73	4.64	4.23	4.56
Readmission within 4 weeks for hemorrhage due to the abortion	11.16	11.27	11.34	10.89	10.19	9.77	9.26	10.72

that induced abortion is responsible for some cases of secondary sterility and cervical incompetence.

DIGGORY: Our next speaker will be Dr. Geijerstam from Stockholm.

GEIJERSTAM: The problem in Scandinavia is more complex than in such countries as Czechoslovakia or Hungary, where most legal abortions are done on healthy women. Most legal abortions in Scandinavia are performed on medical indication and many of the women concerned are in poor health, including some who are very ill indeed. This is one of the reasons for our higher mortality rate. Another cause is that most of the interruptions are done later in pregnancy. We are very well aware of this, and over the last few years there has been a definite trend toward more rapid investigation and earlier abortion (Table 8).

I shall limit myself to a brief report on about 6,200 legal abortions by intrauterine injection of hypertonic saline solution (see Table 9). These data were collected by Professor Bengtsson in Lund. As you can see, a little less than half were done intra-amniotically and a little more than half extra-amniotically. The results with the two methods are quite comparable inasmuch as the procedure was in most cases successful after one injection.

The interval between the injection and the expulsion or surgical evacuation of the fetus was 2.5 days for the intra-amniotic injections and 2.7 days for extra-amniotic injections. There were two deaths after intra-amniotic injection. One of these deaths was not considered to be due to the method; this was a woman who after the

Table 8 Duration of Investigation and Period of Gestation at Legal Abortion: University Hospital, Umea, Sweden, 1963–1967

Year	Number of Abortions	Days of Investigation (median)	Weeks of Gestation (median)
1963–1964	45	25.8	16.0
1965	61	23.3	14.5
1966	96	15.5	13.5
1967	127	11.6	12.6

Table 9 Experience with Legal Abortions by Intrauterine
Injection of Hypertonic Saline Solution

	Intra-amniotic	*Extra-amniotic*
Number of cases	2,797	3,364
Per cent aborting after one injection	96.7	88.5
Days between injection and expulsion or removal of fetus	2.5	2.7
Per cent with P.I.D.	1.6	2.3
Per cent with major hemorrhage	7.8	5.0
Number of deaths	2	1

injection experienced premature separation from the placenta, which
made cesarean section necessary. The woman died from heart failure
during the operation. The other death was due to a too large amount
of hypertonic saline. No less than 400 ml of 20 per cent saline was
injected, which makes about 80 grams of sodium chloride—much too
large a dose to be given in connection with this operation.

The extra-amniotic injection caused one death, which was due to
sepsis. All in all, our experience in Sweden with this method has
been somewhat discouraging. I think I should also mention that all
such two-stage operations are psychologically extremely trying for
the woman.

DIGGORY: The time has now come to throw this discussion open to
the audience.

SCHWARZ: I would make a strong plea for a collaborative prospective
investigation of morbidity, early and late, associated with abortions
performed in hospitals, considering the various methods as well as
the period of gestation. Such data are not yet available, and it seems
to me that several of the groups represented here are well qualified
to undertake this kind of research.

AKINLA: I just want to add very briefly that I have been greatly
surprised that of all of the people that have spoken, nobody has
mentioned mortality from tetanus. I am quite sure that that the
tetanus bacillus is not peculiar to Nigeria. I have surveyed 64
abortions. This number included 34 cases of tetanus, and 19 women
died, a mortality of 56 per cent.

CERNOCH: In our country we have had two cases of tetanus, but only in criminal abortions, none in legal abortions.

NOVAK: In Slovenia, I remember one case of tetanus during the last ten years; it was the result of a criminal abortion.

ABORTION AND CONSTITUTIONALITY

The Means of Assessing and Testing the Constitutionality of Abortion Law in the United States

Harriet F. Pilpel, LL.B. (moderator)
Zad Leavy, LL.B., LL.M. (rapporteur)
Ralph J. Gampell, LL.B.
B. J. George, Jr., J.D.
Roy Lucas, J.D.
Cyril C. Means, Jr., J.D., LL.M.
Eugene Quay, LL.B.
Herman Schwartz, LL.B.

PILPEL: When we discuss constitutionality, we should bear in mind two aspects: (1) the possibility of the laws being declared unconstitutional, and (2) the fact that just bringing test cases, and the dialogue and debate which result, may be extremely helpful. And experience, I think, has proven that challenging the constitutionality of laws, even if the cases are lost, tends to have a public educational effect, and often induces the legislature to do something which otherwise it might not do, as in the New York privacy cases. Or such cases may dispense with the necessity of legislation as in the birth-control cases, or they may impel the repeal of legislation, as with the Connecticut birth-control case.

So whether or not we are eventually successful in declaring clauses unconstitutional in this area, the fact that attacks are mounted and the public is educated as to the infirmities in the laws will become, I think, extremely useful.

We have arranged this session so that each speaker will have a very short, much too short, time in which to develop his position. First, Mr. Means will talk about the constitutionality of the laws and the historical background.

MEANS: At common law no abortion was a crime, no matter what means was used to induce it, if performed before quickening and with the woman's consent. Surgical abortions before quickening were first prohibited by Lord Ellenborough's Act in 1803, and next by a section of the New York Revised Statutes of 1829 (enacted in 1828).

I have found practically no contemporary evidence of the legislative intent behind the English Act of 1803, but fortunately such evidence does exist—though I am revealing it now for the first time since its long forgotten publication 140 years ago—in regard to the New York legislation of 1828, which was the earliest Anglo-American statute containing an express therapeutic exception, justifying an abortion if "necessary to preserve the life of such mother."

In their report to the legislature of October 15, 1828, the New York Revisers (Benjamin Franklin Butler [1795–1858] and John Caulfield Spencer [1788–1855]) described this unprecedented express therapeutic exception as "just and necessary."[1] Their use of the word "necessary" both in their report and in their statute obviously alludes to the ethical doctrine that necessity justifies therapeutic feticide recognized by most Christian theologians since Tertullian (c. 160–c. 220) and never condemned by any Christian body before the Holy Office decrees of May 31, 1884, August 19, 1889, and July 24, 1895. But it was in another section which the Revisers proposed, but the legislature did not adopt, that they left the clue to the rationale of their section on abortion, and of its therapeutic exception.

That other proposed but unpassed section deals with surgical operations other than abortion. It read:

Every person who shall perform any surgical operation, by which human life shall be destroyed or endangered, such as the amputation of a limb, or of the breast, trepanning, cutting for the stone, or for hernia, unless it appear that the same was necessary for the preservation of life, or was advised, by at least two physicians, shall be adjudged guilty of a misdemeanor.[2]

In their note to this proposed section the Revisers explained:

The rashness of many young practitioners in performing the most important surgical operations for the mere purpose of distinguishing themselves, has

---

[1] Report of the Commissioners Appointed to Revise the Statute Laws of this State made to the Legislature October 15, 1828, p. 74, ad § 24 (renumbered § 21 by the Legislature), in 6 The Original Reports of the Different Chapters Composing the Revised Statutes as Presented to the Legislature by the Revisers (Albany 1827 and 1828).

[2] Ibid., note 9, at p. 75, § 28.

been a subject of much complaint, and we are advised by old and experienced surgeons, that the loss of life occasioned by the practice, is alarming.[3]

This precious and long unpublished text tells us volumes about the danger of surgery—*all* surgery, not just surgical abortion—140 years ago. Almost 40 years would still elapse before, in 1867, Joseph Lister would publish in *The Lancet* his discovery of antiseptic surgery. Until that future innovation became general, every surgical operation endangered the patient's life and health, through the possibility of infection which surgeons did not understand and could not control. Therefore only a patient medically advised that his chance of surviving the operation exceeded his chance of surviving the condition the operation would remove was given a choice between the two alternatives. Not only abortion, but every kind of surgery, was eschewed by responsible physicians, except where really necessary to save the patient's life.

The legislature adopted the Revisers' first proposal, to prohibit nontherapeutic abortion, but not their second proposal, to prohibit other types of nontherapeutic surgery. Why not? Not because the legislature disagreed with the Revisers' stated reasons for their second proposal; in 1828 no sensible man could have disagreed with those. The difference in legislative reaction to the two proposals was doubtless due to the following consideration: in respect of every operation except abortion, a combination of patient's caution and practitioner's conscience sufficed to prevent unnecessary surgery. As the *New York Times* warned in 1863, it was only in regard to abortion that extreme social and economic pressures often drove "thoughtless women, . . . rash mortals, into an undesirable eternity." In the case of abortion alone, therefore, did the legislators of 1828 deem necessary a new provision in the penal law.

The English and New York Acts of 1803 and 1828, forbidding surgical abortion before quickening, broke the ground. Before 1850, eleven more American states had followed suit. Only one of these nineteenth-century statutes ever received a judicial construction by a contemporary court explaining why it had been passed: the New Jersey Act of March 1, 1849. In 1858, in *State v. Murphy*, the old

[3]Ibid.

Supreme Court of New Jersey, in a unanimous opinion written by one of America's greatest judges, Chief Justice (afterward Chancellor) Henry Woodhull Green, declared: "The design of the statute was not to prevent the procuring of abortions, so much as to guard the health and life of the mother against the consequences of such attempts." (State v. Murphy, 27 N.J.L. 112, 114–115 [Sup. Ct. 1858]). Of the three associate justices who joined their chief in this opinion, one was Daniel Haines. He had been the governor of New Jersey who, on March 1, 1849, had approved and signed the very statute which this opinion, nine years later, construed.

The New York Revisers' Report of 1828 and the New Jersey decision of 1858 in *State v. Murphy* are literally the only known contemporary authoritative texts explaining the reason for the enactment of any of these novel prohibitions of surgical abortion before quickening. Both point to the life and health of the pregnant woman as the sole object in legislative view.

The common law protected the quickened (but not the unquickened) fetus as a being with its own right to life, immune to destruction at maternal will. By prohibiting surgical as well as nonsurgical destruction of an unquickened fetus, the new statutes, beginning in 1803 and 1828, could easily be mistaken as intending to confer a similar right and immunity upon the early fetus. That this was not the legislative intention, however, is demonstrated by the fact that the statutes of New York enacted at the same time, and still in force today, permit the execution of a pregnant woman under sentence of death, authorizing her reprieve only if the fetus has quickened.

The new statutes were inspired by reverence for life, but the life they revered was the pregnant woman's, not that of the unquickened fetus. All they intended to do—and this they did intend—was to protect the health and lives of women with unwanted pregnancies from damage and destruction by abortion, an operation which in their day, even when performed on healthy women in hospitals, produced greater maternal mortality than childbirth. This was inevitably so because, unlike normal delivery, every surgical abortion requires the insertion of instruments into the womb; in an age when surgeons did not sterilize their instruments one requires little imagination to picture the consequences.

Thanks to Lord Lister and many others of his profession, both the abortient and the parturient rates of maternal mortality have now sunk to infinitesimal fractions of what they were 140 years ago. But this reduction in their absolute values is not the only change; there has also been a reversal in their relative magnitudes. That which was higher—the rate of maternal mortality suffered by healthy women in consequence of hospital abortions—now is lower. Today it is safer for a healthy woman to have an early hospital abortion than to bear a child in the same hospital.

Figure 1 is a schematic diagram in which curve PP' represents the parturient rate of maternal mortality during the past 140 years, and curve AA' represents the abortient rate of maternal mortality (which equals the rate of maternal mortality of healthy women aborted in hospitals). Both curves begin to descend after Lister's inauguration of antiseptic surgery (1867). At some point (designated 19??) before 1950, when the first statistically significant universes of data on healthy women aborted in hospitals early in pregnancy became available, the more rapidly descending curve AA' intersected and passed (and remains) below curve PP'. 19?? is therefore the date which marks a constitutional watershed in regard to these nine-teenth-century compulsory gestation statutes. Before 19??, their

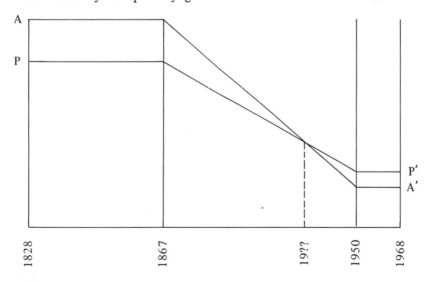

Figure 1

enforcement continued to effectuate their original purpose: to compel women to choose the safer of two alternatives—childbirth rather than even a hospital abortion. After 19??, continued enforcement of these laws not only did not serve their original purpose, it also frustrated their original purpose, by compelling women to choose the less safe of the two alternatives (childbirth).

Not only common-law rules, but prohibitory statutes and even prohibitions embedded in state constitutions have been stricken down by courts which applied the Roman legal maxim, *Cessante ratione legis, cessat et ipsa lex* (When the reason for a law ceases, the law itself also ceases). If ever statute deserved that fate, it is the just dessert of these now obsolete compulsory gestation laws.

The cases declaring prohibitory statutes and even state constitutional provisions obsolete under this Roman legal maxim apply it, of course, as a norm of statutory construction, rather than as a criterion of continued constitutionality. I know of no decision that has used it as a touchstone for the latter purpose, at least none that has done this explicitly. I venture to think, however, that a responsible and responsive court could be persuaded to do so where, as here, penal statutes that were passed to shield women from danger to health and life are now, even when obeyed, a sword endangering their health and life. *Cessante ratione constitutionalitatis, cessat et ipsa constitutionalitas.*

PILPEL: Our next speaker will be Mr. Leavy, who will address himself to the question of constitutional rights of women involved in an abortion situation.

LEAVY: The right of a woman to maintain her physical and mental health, the right of a woman to maintain, if not improve, the quality of her life and that of her family, including her existing children, are rights which today she may not successfully assert. Stated conversely, she is commanded, under penalty of imprisonment, to bear and raise a child which she does not want; she is commanded to bear and raise a child which perhaps nobody wants, condemned for life as a burden upon society. She is commanded to follow and adhere to a religious and moral philosophy which may mean little to her under the circumstances. She is commanded to refrain from using a means of birth control in family planning which is and has been the single most widely used method at least since the beginning of man's recorded history, a method which is now perfectly safe and accepted medically and scientifically.

We could go on with different variations on the same theme. But, in a capsule, I submit to you that if there are any substantial prohibitions against abortion, then the state, in making the crucial decision for the woman and for her family, takes something of value from her without due process of law. This is in violation of the Fourteenth Amendment, and perhaps the Ninth Amendment, to the United States Constitution, and also in violation of the various state constitutions.

The state as a practical matter denies the woman equal protection of law. If she is poor, she will not receive adequate treatment. If she has money, she will be able to obtain the clandestine abortion she would not be able to get if she were poor.

The state invades the woman's privacy and that of her family when it makes the crucial decision for her that she must bear the child. As stated in *Griswold v. Connecticut* (381 U.S. 479, 1965), which you have heard much about at this conference, there are certain zones of privacy into which the state may not intrude. The *Griswold* case held Connecticut's anticontraception laws to be an unconstitutional invasion of these zones of personal privacy, and we believe that the law of abortion will come within this concept.

The state's presence and intrusion, by virtue of the prohibitory law, is drastic and oppressive, especially with respect to the one million or more women in this country who resort to illegal abortions each year. For the state to exercise its police power in this drastic and oppressive way, there must be some legitimate reason to do so. There must be some valid interest which serves the people of the state in order to intrude so drastically into the woman's life.

What can the state's interest be? To preserve morals, that is, to deter illicit intercourse, perhaps? I think this argument hardly deserves the dignity of our discussion here in the light of existing case law to the contrary. To preserve the health of women by deterring them from clandestine abortion? If that is the interest served by this prohibitory law, I submit that it has been an abysmal failure for centuries, since the beginning of man's social life on this earth. The prohibitory abortion law has been the most widely violated law in man's history. Boldly stated, it drives the desperate woman right into the hands of the person from which it is designed to protect her—the unskilled abortionist. The effect of existing law is to perpetuate a public health problem of epidemic proportions.

Is there an interest on the part of the state in protecting some right of embryo or fetus to be born? I submit to you that now we come into the realm of opinion. Scientific facts are manipulated to buttress opinions sanctified by moral and religious rationale. But I suggest to you that the anti-abortion moral and religious philosophy has its deepest roots in the basic drive of man to increase his numbers.

I suggest to you that the population motive, which might well have been considered a legitimate state interest in past years, under other circumstances, manifests itself today not only in the religious and moral rationale, but as well in the breast of male ego. It is the male who raises the armies and the work force. It is the male who resists any intrusion or change in the reproductive cycle which he has initiated. But the population motive in this day and age can no longer be a legitimate state interest. Indeed, the population motive is a threat to mankind.

Whatever state interest there may be is miniscule compared with the oppressiveness of the state's intrusion into the private life of the woman, and of the interposition of the state's presence between the woman and her doctor.

How will women receive recognition of their rights? I believe we are going to see recognition in the courts before we see it in the legislatures. From what we have seen thus far, in any event, it may be accomplished by various approaches. One is declaratory relief, as Mr. Lucas has brought to our attention already, i.e., a decision compelling a hospital to provide the same kind of care to poor people as to the rich and the middle class. Another is in the area of negligence and malpractice, where a doctor or a hospital has refused to terminate a pregnancy contrary to the accepted standards of medical practice, and there are serious consequences and damages. As we saw in *Griswold v. Connecticut*, changes may come in a criminal abortion case, and one is now pending before the California Supreme Court (People v. Belous, 1969). Women's rights also could be recognized in disciplinary actions against physicians, such as the San Francisco Doctors' Cases, where rubella abortions were performed in good faith.

I would hopefully predict that the courts will conclude one way or another that perhaps the best position for the state is to stay out of the abortion business, and leave the decision to the woman and her physician, acting within the realm of proper medical practice, as stated by Father Robert Drinan, a prominent priest and dean of the Boston College Law School.

I suggest to you, in conclusion, that if, as has been reported, there are 100,000 women each year, for example, in the state of California who are going to get abortions one way or the other, and if there are some hospitals in that state which will admit these women for this treatment, and if there are some doctors in that state who will do the operation, then I suggest that whatever your feelings are on abortion, to deny the woman the elemental standard of minimal medical care, that is, the right to have surgery in a hospital and have a doctor in attendance, is a denial of a fundamental and basic right in violation of due process of law.

PILPEL: Because of the time limitations none of the lawyers tonight will cite supporting authorities. But it seems safe to say that there are cases and statutes and treatises to support the arguments being made, so that you should understand that this is not simply what the panelists are saying. This is their considered judgment after examination of the relevant precedents.

Our next speaker is a man known both as Dr. Gampell and Mr. Gampell, for the simple reason he is both a doctor and a lawyer. He is therefore extremely able to present our next subject division, which has to do with the rights of the physician.

GAMPELL: Essentially, what I am going to do is think out loud, because I don't think that there is any real body of law to which we can look. The first analysis is a simple one: If we can find constitutionally protected rights of the woman, then by definition there are constitutionally protected derivative rights of the doctor, it being self-evident that she cannot have an abortion unless some doctor is there to do it. Therefore, her right cannot be protected without protecting the right of the doctor.

But the question is whether or not there is any constitutionally protected right of the doctor standing alone. A starting point might be the proposition that the state has a legitimate interest in regulating the practice of medicine in order to protect the health of its population. And I believe that this goes beyond licensing and general regulatory provisions.

A good example might be the state's power to stop the use by doctors of quack cancer cures. I don't doubt, for example, that in my own state of California there are licensed physicians who genuinely believe that Krebiozin and drugs of that nature are legitimate modalities for treatment of cancer. Nevertheless, after an expert determination—and I would urge that phrase on you—after an expert determination, the state, in the exercise of its police power, has made it illegal for a physician to use that kind of treatment.

Now, I think the converse is equally true, that, if the state is persuaded that after expert examination a course of treatment is medically indicated, then the state should not interpose its police power to prevent that treatment, and the doctor has a constitutionally protected right to administer that treatment.

The state can and should be persuaded that there is a vast majority of educated medical opinion in favor of broadening the indications for abortion, and perhaps even removing all restrictions so as to rely solely on the good faith and determination of physicians to adhere to proper medical standards. Surveys show 80 per cent of doctors in favor of liberalizing abortion laws, with many doctors in favor of removing all state intervention.

Now, I don't wish to step over into somebody else's field, but in analyzing the position of the doctor I think that the vagueness doctrine must be at least looked into. It is all very well to say that the void-for-vagueness thrust goes to the woman, and this is one of her grounds for seeking constitutional relief. But the void-for-vagueness doctrine can send a doctor to a penitentiary, and this is a good deal more pertinent.

The general statement of the doctrine is that a statute which either forbids or requires the doing of an act in terms so vague that men of common intelligence must necessarily guess as to its meaning and differ as to its application, violates the first essential of due process.

The courts recognize that the vague statute requires the actor to proceed at his peril and, hence, has the effect of throttling protective conditions; that is, even if the action is legitimate, the doctor won't do it for fear of getting into trouble. Now remember that the doctor here can be a two-time loser with the vague anti-abortion law. If he guesses wrong he can go to jail by way of criminal prosecution. Then in the civil courts he can be sued for not doing it, which is the *Gleitman v. Cosgrove* case (49 N.J. 22, 1967), or he can be sued for doing it under the assault and battery theory. (If it is criminal it cannot be consented to, ergo, it is an assault.)

Luckily my state is bright enough not to go along with this. In California the abortee may not sue the abortionist, but I understand that this is the minority view. If you are in the majority jurisdictions, however, you literally can be a two-time loser. You are damned if you do and damned if you don't.

So it seems to me that a doctor has the right to say that it is constitutionally wrong for him to have to practice his profession at such a peril, and, therefore, he can seek declaratory or other relief on constitutional grounds.

I don't think these arguments will sway a state supreme court in the near future. We may be a distance away, but the arguments should be made in order to give the courts the legal theories on which they ultimately may clarify the law in a progressive way. One: The vagueness doctrine. Secondly: The converse of the regulatory power to interdict, that is, after a good showing having been made, the state has a duty to permit action.

PILPEL: It is interesting to note that in the Connecticut birth control case (Griswold v. Conn., 381 U.S. 479, 1965) the majority does talk in terms of the state interfering with the intimate and private relations of husband and wife, and with one aspect of that relation, their confidentiality with their physician. So I would suggest that might be a possible basis for attacking the constitutionality of the anti-abortion laws.

GAMPELL: If you will look to the magic words of Mr. Justice Douglas in the *Griswold* case, where he said that the constitutionality "operates directly on the intimate relation of husband and wife, and their physician's role in one aspect of that relationship," it may be that he is delineating an independent right of the physician. But I am not sure that he is.

PILPEL: That is what I suggested: I think he is. At least it is possible that he is delineating an independent right of the physician.

We have discussed the historical background of the laws, and the rights of women in an abortion situation, and the rights of the physician. We've heard much about the fact that there has been insufficient attention paid to the rights of a third entity, and a lot of discussion as to whether that entity is indeed a person. Mr. Quay will address himself to the question of the constitutionality of the laws with reference to the rights of the fetus.

QUAY: The basic rights of the fetus are the same as yours and mine and are protected by the same constitutional safeguards. A consideration often overlooked in discussions of this kind is the original purpose of abortion laws, which were repressive, not permissive. Laws against homicide could not be applied to a killing prior to the only point, "quickening," at which life could be legally established. But destruction of even a potential life was condemned.

Nor was this legal emphasis on the right to life weakened by the exception which allows abortion to save the mother's life. Here, too, the sanctity of life was written in when the state of medical science was such that the choice was not between the life of the mother and the life of the child. It was between the life of the mother or the death of both. Like the English statute of 1803, the first abortion laws in the United States were not a relaxation of the laws against murder, but created a new crime to fill a gap.

There was no intent of the law to disregard the right of a fetus to life. The law protected this life from the time it was thought to exist as a separate entity, just as it does today. The difference is that science can now tell us that new life begins at the moment of fertilization.

The courts have frequently taken note of this increase in scientific knowledge and incorporated it in their decisions. In Massachusetts it was declared: "The laws presume to keep pace with science, and medical science has certainly made progress since 1884. . . . From the viewpoint of the civil law and the law of property, a child *en ventre sa mère* is not only regarded as a human being, but regarded as such from the moment of conception, which it is in fact." In 1960, the New Jersey Supreme Court made it a matter of law in declaring: "Medical authorities have long recognized that a child is in existence from the moment of conception." And at least one state—Wisconsin—has amended its abortion laws and taken account of the change in scientific thinking, defining "an unborn child" as "a human being from the time of conception until it is born alive."

Courts early determined in cases relating to inheritance or title to property that the fetus must be recognized as a living human being— a person—from the moment of conception. In the great flood of personal injury actions of recent years, this is recognized still further. For example, New Jersey's highest court said: "Medical authorities recognize that before birth an infant is a distinct entity and . . . the law recognizes the rights which he will enjoy when born can be violated before birth." In 1933 Colorado inserted a clause to make express provision for the unborn in its statute relating to dependent children. In another personal injury case, the Ohio Supreme Court ruled that the article of the Ohio Constitution guaranteeing that the courts are open to all persons applied equally to the unborn person. In this case a pregnant woman was injured in a crash and her unborn infant was saved though born prematurely and terribly injured. The Court held that the child in the womb had a distinct life of her own and that an action for damages would lie in her name.

The Fourteenth Amendment to the United States Constitution declared in much the same language as the then-existing state constitutions that no state may "deprive any person of life, liberty or property, without due process of law; nor deny to any person within its jurisdiction the equal protection of the law."

In view of this it would be difficult to defend liberalized abortion laws—past or proposed—against the challenge of unconstitutionality. If such a challenge were made, the courts would be faced with the dilemma of declaring that an unborn child can be a person for some purposes, yet not for others, including the most important one of the right to life, or else holding the new abortion laws unconstitutional, as indeed I believe them to be.

In reading the new statutes, one must be struck by the near uniformity with which conditions for legalized abortion are prescribed, with no provision for enforcement of these conditions. There is no tribunal in the usual sense, no judge, no jury, and no attorney provided to see that the conditions of the statutes are met and the limitations preserved. No standards are set for testing the indications for abortion. So, all is left to one or several medical men, who are required to give no more than a "substantial opinion" that the individual case does in reality meet the requirements of the law, whereas in a proceeding before a real tribunal, the doctors would have to appear as expert witnesses and would be required not only to give the basis for their opinion, but to defend it under cross-examination.

Second, such statutes would be an attempt at an unconstitutional delegation of judicial authority to private individuals. Of such, the North Carolina Supreme Court stated in 1953: "The Legislature cannot vest in a subordinate agency the power to apply or withhold the application of the law in its absolute unguided discretion."

Third, and most glaring of all, is the failure of such statutes to provide a hearing for the child in the womb. The proceeding is completely *ex parte* with not even nominal representation for the one who in this type of action must be regarded as the defendant. The medical men alone determine on the killing of the child *in utero* and follow that decision by executing the sentence they have imposed. Contrast this with the principles laid down in the famous Scottsboro case of 1932, in which the United States Supreme Court held that seven Negroes, ignorant, illiterate, yet forced to stand trial without counsel, had been denied due process. The Court stated:

Let us suppose the extreme case of a prisoner charged with a capital offense who is deaf and dumb, illiterate and feeble minded, unable to employ counsel, with the whole power of the State arrayed against him, prosecuted by counsel for the State without assignment of counsel for the defense, tried, convicted and sentenced to death. Such a result, which, if carried into execution, would be little short of judicial murder, would be a gross violation of the guarantee of due process of law; and we venture to think that no appellate court, State or Federal, would hesitate so to decide. . . .

The revised abortion statutes are equally defective in regard to substantive aspects of due process which restrict legislative enactment of unfair and unjust laws. That the due process clause is binding on legislative action is made abundantly clear by numerous federal and state rulings. To be brief, I will cite none until the discussion.

One common assertion is that as a matter of "civil right" every woman has such use or disposition of her own body as she pleases. As noted above it has been ruled that the child in the womb is not a part of the mother. But aside from this, it should be noted that if such a right could be established without regard for how it might affect other individuals or a community, it would be necessary to repeal many other laws such as those against prostitution, drug abuse, and indecent exposure, as well as various compulsory health measures.

In any case, a mother's assertion of her right to abortion was coldly received by the New Jersey Supreme Court. In a 1967 decision, the court stated:

The right to life is inalienable in our society. . . . We are not faced with the necessity of balancing the mother's life against that of her child. The sanctity of the single human life is the decisive factor in this suit in court. . . . It may have been easier for the mother and less expensive for the father to have terminated the life of their child while he was an embryo, but these alleged detriments cannot stand against the preciousness of the single human life to support a remedy in court. Though we sympathize with the unfortunate situation in which these parents find themselves, we firmly believe the right of the child to live is greater than and precludes their right not to endure emotional and financial injury.

This reasoning seems to me applicable to the entire abortion problem. On the one hand we have the principle of the inalienable right to life universally upheld by our courts. On the other are the advocates of liberalized abortion who ask all of us to allow abrogation of this right for reasons small in comparison with what is given up. The choice, then, is between a speculative, temporary relief for a relative handful, and the retention of our most cherished constitutional safeguards. As we have seen, those changes could be made, if at all, only by constitutional amendments. Could we do this and still maintain the basic structure of our law?

It must never be forgotten that all the rights of which Americans are so proud rest upon constitutional safeguards. Abandon these, or permit them to be eroded, and we will have unwittingly substituted a state in which those rights can be conceded or withheld at the will of either a majority or an effective minority. Such a change would leave all of us at the mercy of some future Hitler. And any group whose continued existence might seem at the time a social or economic liability would be faced, perhaps under the guise of the latest in human engineering, with the prospect of another Dachau.

PILPEL: It is clear that there are two sides hotly contesting the constitutional issue and that they devolve upon the same question which started this conference, namely, whether the fetus is a person.

Our next speaker is Professor Herman Schwartz, who is from Buffalo, but presently is at Michigan Law School. He will address himself to the question touched on by Dr. Gampell—the question of vagueness as a ground for attacking the constitutionality of the anti-abortion statutes.

SCHWARTZ: Let me just mention some phrases that may be regarded as unduly vague. One is "impairment of physical or mental health." Another one is "to preserve life." These are the more specific ones. And Dr. Overstreet this morning pointed out that these aren't exactly clear beacon lights.

Another phrase, which appears in the Pennsylvania and New Jersey laws, is "without lawful justification."

In connection with these so-called guidelines or standards, there was something touched upon by Mr. Quay which struck me as probably one of the few points he made that I can agree with, and that is the problem of vagueness involved in an excessive delegation of power. Mr. Gampell read the classic statement by Justice Holmes in the McBoyle case, which has appeared in a number of free-speech cases; and the important thing about the vagueness notion is that not only are the parties unable to know what is right or wrong, but in order to avoid risking anything they move very far away from what might be right.

Now, the result here is that the person who is directly affected, namely, the prospective abortee, really doesn't have much to say about this decision to move far away from the line of illegality or legality. In other areas, such as in obscenity cases, where a person's own financial interests are involved, he will risk moving close to the line. But the person involved here is the doctor; it is the doctor who will be prosecuted. The woman rarely is. The result is that the doctor has less of an incentive to risk anything.

This becomes especially acute when you have medical committees, when it isn't even their patient involved. In these medical committees the deciding factor may be the staff administrator of the hospital, who is even further removed from the patient. There is a chilling effect on a basic right, and regardless of which way one comes out on it, one cannot deny that what is involved here is terribly basic, the kind of life a woman and her family are going to lead.

Alan Guttmacher has written of an interesting experience he had when he was a young doctor. He went to the District Attorney and said: "Can I perform an abortion?" and the District Attorney said, "Of course not, but I won't investigate. I will not do anything under those circumstances."

This brings me to the more subtle question, and one of the most difficult, which I am sure Professor George will elaborate on—equal protection of the law. This is a problem of excessive discretion. One of the dangers of a vague statute is that it is not enforced uniformly by the people who have the business of enforcing it, and this includes prosecutors, juries, judges, and, in a sense, the hospital therapeutic abortion committees.

Doctors have enormous discretion over what they are going to do, and they tend toward conservatism in the face of publicity given to restrictive views of a vague law. This happened in New Jersey, where the Court said, "You can't have an abortion for rubella." So the Attorney General immediately called a meeting of all the prosecutors and said, "We will construe this administratively in such-and-such a way." That is fine, but it shouldn't depend on an administrator to construe an uncertain law. Suppose one of them decides to break the agreement, or a new prosecutor comes into the picture. There is very little control over this kind of thing, and the doctor is not sure where he stands.

The danger present is that of retroactivity. What you had in

California and New Jersey and elsewhere is that a lot of doctors went along assuming that abortions for rubella were justifiable, and suddenly the State Medical Board said, "No." You then have the danger of ex post facto illegality for what they thought was being done properly.

The police are also involved in interpreting a vague statute. After the Bourne case in England, the doctors seemed to think that they could perform abortions. But there was a report in the *New York Times* about one doctor who said that before the new legislation was passed, although he was performing legal abortions, he would frequently get visits from policemen. This can be a very serious harrassment, I gather.

Now, among the more serious dangers involved with interpreting a vague law is the difference between the prosecutor who will and the one who won't prosecute. And there is the problem of excessive emotional feelings involved in interpreting the phrase, "to preserve life." It's difficult to be objective in making decisions on this basis and most of the statutes, both old and new, don't involve any review of the hospital committees.

So, in effect, the medical profession is left completely at sea to use it own judgment, and, as Dr. Overstreet indicated, some doctors are a little more punitive than others and some a little more liberal than others. There is no way of reviewing this.

What if the woman is arbitrarily turned down? If she has a recourse, what standards should be used to attack the judgment? My time is up and I must quit in midstream.

PILPEL: Maybe you will have a chance to answer questions.

These various grounds of constitutionality, or lack thereof, are submitted for consideration. They might be used cumulatively or separately. In discussing them no speaker is attempting to say that there is only one ground; a constitutionality attack is usually mounted on as many grounds as possible.

SCHWARTZ: Incidentally, another factor is that often you can make an attack on a state constitution, since it sometimes has its own wrinkles, such as separation of powers, which can be picked up.

Some novel ideas can be carried in a state court which might not get anywhere in a federal court.

PILPEL: Our next speaker will address himself to a different part of the Fourteenth Amendment. Professor George recently was at the University of Michigan School of Law, and is now with the Practicing Law Institute in New York. He will discuss the abortion laws in connection with the concept of equal protection of the laws.

GEORGE: Mr. Quay included the text of the Fourteenth Amendment, equal protection of laws. It was historically an effort by the Reconstruction Congress to assure equality for the former slaves. Because of a restrictive interpretation by the Supreme Court, not too many years after it was passed, it fell largely into disuse until fairly recently. It has loomed large in many of the antisegregation cases, and I suppose in that sense, it is finally fulfilling the intent of its original drafters. But it has also been invoked, I think, very often as a "make weight" in attacks on legislation and on administrative activity.

Working as I do from the context of the criminal law and procedure, its chief application seems to be in terms of unwarranted charges of faults in a statute, either in terms of what is included or what is excluded. Not too often, incidentally, has a substantive criminal statute been successfully attacked on this ground.

The second application is when a procedure militates against the indigent it will be reached under the equal protection clause. I find it possible to urge that the equal protection clause might, for example, be invoked to reach the inequality of prohibiting abortion on socioeconomic grounds while allowing it for eugenic, humanitarian, and therapeutic indications.

I can see also some possibilities, in the abstract, of it being used to attack the provisions that can be administered only in hospitals available to those with funds, thus making abortion in fact unavailable to the indigent, who must go to public clinics, where abortion is rare.

Judging from the materials gathered and presented to this conference and others, however, I find myself, I think, basically in disagreement with Mr. Leavy. I view the opportunities to use this equal-protection type of argument, or any of these other arguments, to be wholly fortuitous.

Forgive me if I trespass a bit on Mr. Lucas's emphasis, but being a procedure man I can't stay away from this. If you try to envision what kind of a person would be in a position procedurally to invoke these ideas, the most beneficial one would be the one that Mr. Leavy is involved in: A disciplinary action against a physician whose livelihood is at stake, where you are attacking an administrative agency on procedural due process grounds, and also on the legitimacy of the standards being invoked; where you can muster a large number of interested doctors to contribute to the expenses of litigation, which is not a boon to be lightly dismissed. Unfortunately, however, there is seldom any disciplinary action against physicians who have not already been convicted in the criminal courts as abortionists. It is fairly evident that doctors working through hospital teams are not being reached under the criminal abortion statutes. That leaves two classes of people who might be interested, the licensed (or unlicensed but skilled) physician operating outside a hospital, and the woman herself.

With respect to the physician, I do not see any court in this decade invoking due process and equal protection concepts for the benefit of one who probably will be viewed, at least for public consumption, as a pariah by his own profession. This is not an appealing sort of client to present for an equal-protection argument.

With respect to the woman, knowing what I do about the processes of the law, if she isn't pregnant, she's not likely to be listened to on the basis that she might be pregnant and wish an abortion. That is not a good class to set up under Federal Rule 23. Or if she is pregnant, by the time we get through the pretrial hearing, the infant will be six months of age.

So, as a practical possibility, you are not too likely to assert these various ideas successfully. All this leads me still to believe that if you have informed public opinion, of which a judge might have become aware, you may have the basis for proceeding in the legislative channels. My emphasis would be here in the hope that if we can make one advance this year or next year—for example, the ALI type of statute—it may be possible a decade hence to get what I personally would like to see, and that is abortion being considered a medical matter like any other, having to do with the patient as a total person.

PILPEL: Our last speaker has kindly consented to pull together a variety of subject matters which didn't fit under the subjects of any of the preceding speakers. Mr. Lucas will address himself, among other things, to the constitutional attacks that might be mounted in terms of freedom of association and separation of church and state, and will say a few words, I trust, in answer to Professor George, as to why he thinks that a case could be successfully mounted.

LUCAS: I think while Professor George's argument is still warm I should express my disagreement with it. His argument is that a class of physicians who are deterred from exercising their best medical judgment would not be able to go into court and obtain a declaratory judgment that the anti-abortion statutes are unconstitutional. This is a procedural issue before you even get to the issue of whether or not the statute is unconstitutional.

On the contrary, however, recent cases indicate that the Supreme Court is taking very definite strides away from the idea that a person has to be imminently threatened with prosecution before he has standing to go into court and sue.

We had a case last year involving drug manufacturers. I think that the name of the case, for the record, was *Abbott Laboratories v. Gardner*. Certain drug manufacturers were not yet facing criminal prosecution, but they were allowed to go ahead and challenge the constitutional validity of those statutes.

We had a declaratory relief case decided just last week, involving a law which has been on the books in Arkansas for the last thirty years—not as serious a question as abortion, but the question of whether or not public teachers can teach Darwin's theory of evolution. Six years ago, when *Poe v. Ulman* was decided the other way, the wrong way, the Supreme Court might have ruled differently in the Arkansas evolution case. It might have said that this statute has been on the books a long time, and there is no threat of enforcement since the woman had moved out of Arkansas. But they didn't do that. Nine justices decided that the controversy was there before the Court and they would go ahead and decide it because of the possible impact of the statute being on the books.

There is no doubt that you can document the serious impact of contemporary abortion statutes on the physicians who from day to day must make decisions in anticipation of how the law may be interpreted. That is what we would base our claim on, that you can show a recurring need of physicians to decide whether or not an abortion is legal, and you can show that they turn away many patients, and that their practice would be quite different if the law were clearer or more liberal in allowing greater latitude in medical judgment. We may rise or fall on that point, but we do have a good chance of success.

I might point out that one thing we are trying to do in this panel is to develop general theories which fit somehow into the Constitution, into the Bill of Rights, theories which will enable us to say that there is some basic interest to be protected from the state's intrusion, some basic right being asserted here, which will prevail unless overridden by a valid, reasonable, and compelling state interest which has greater weight.

Briefly, we have addressed ourselves to setting up these basic rights. Now, the two that I am going to talk about are freedom of association and the separation of church and state, neither of which I regard as our best arguments, but one never can tell what might be the best arguments when they get to the Supreme Court.

The independent arguments that have been made about physicians and patients can be combined or, shall we say, reformulated into a hypothesis that the typical state abortion laws violate some freedom of association. This is an expression the Supreme Court used originally in the cases involving the NAACP and its right as a political association, as a group, distinct from the rights of individual members of the group. The potentialities of this argument are not very great, although they have been tried in one case, as mentioned briefly in various articles.

But two forms of personal association are implicit in any situation where a request for termination of pregnancy is made. The first is the association of husband and wife, which was explicitly recognized in *Griswold*. Similarly, you might have the association of physician and patient, which was also given a certain amount of recognition in

Griswold. Thus I would argue that there is a possibility of our constitutional argument being validly based on freedom of association.

The *Griswold* decision relied very much on the freedom of association cases. Justice Douglas, in his cryptic way, referred to marriage as an association that promotes a way of life, "an association for as noble a purpose as any involved in our prior decisions." What he did was to apply the prior association cases to the association of husband and wife, and physician and patient.

Let me move on and try to point out where this gets us. We can probably get some help in the decisions that apply a freedom of association theory to attorney and client. This is protected conduct, with respect to speech, which is clearly protected in many ways under the Constitution, and it is conduct that we are concerned about. Now, surgery isn't conduct at all, but the attorney-client cases have protected a certain amount of professional conduct and interaction between clients and attorneys. Those might lend us a little bit of weight.

Finally, let me turn to the kinds of constitutional tests which the courts would apply once we were able to establish a presumption that our constitutional claim was valid. They would say something like this: A governmental purpose to control activities which are subject to state regulations, may not be achieved by principles which sweep unnecessarily broadly and thereby invade the area of protected freedoms. This is a key phrase. After that, the courts will talk about a statute having to be narrowed. If, for instance, you are going to try to stop promiscuity, you must work to regulate specific objectionable activities, not just broadly prohibit coeducational schools. The regulatory law has to be specific.

Another test to be applied would be where fundamental personal liberties are involved. They may not be abridged by the state simply upon the showing that a regulatory statute has some rational relationship to the effectuation of the broadly stated purpose. Where there is a significant encroachment upon personal liberty, the state may prevail only upon showing a subordinating interest which is compelling. That is a proposition upon which the case may turn, particularly when you have large numbers of people excluded from the new ALI-type statutes now being enacted (e.g., Colorado and

North Carolina), to wit, that their interest is fundamental and the state's justification for leaving them out is not.

Now, I will try to summarize the separation of church and state position. This is perhaps the final argument which can be raised, that the laws regulating abortion are laws respecting an establishment of religion. The quickest way to sum this up is to show that the abortion restrictions arise out of a metaphysical theory that the fertilized ovum is a human being entitled to the protection of ultimate birth and life. But in the same sense, all of the statements in the Decalogue can be said both to be religious and to represent some state interest.

The chief obstacle to knocking out the abortion laws on the establishment of religion point, even though you can prove that maintenance of the laws is religiously motivated, is the argument of the other side that there is a state interest in protecting the sanctity of life. This is an argument not easily dismissed.

PILPEL: There is another argument we haven't mentioned yet: That the abortion laws represent the infliction of cruel and unusual punishment in violation of the Ninth Amendment. This should not be lost sight of in the welter of constitutional positions presented here.

I am sorry we couldn't do a more thorough job, but I think we have skirted at least the top of the constitutional arguments which could be made.

Would the panel like to say anything further?

GRANFIELD: I would like to ask Professor George a question. What do you think are the strongest constitutional grounds for attacking newly enacted, more liberal laws?

GEORGE: My approach is really less a doctrinal one than it is an effort to try to assay pragmatically.

GRANFIELD: That is what I want, the pragmatic.

GEORGE: The attitude of the courts will depend upon the type of case. Whether you have a good defense will depend on whether you have a class action, or whether somebody is moving against the doctor, loaded with beautiful arguments for one side.

Mention is made of the contraceptives case, yet you must bear in mind that we had only about two or three states that purported to regulate contraception. We had very widespread and acknowledged practice in terms of contraceptive use and contraceptive advice. These statutes were viewed as an anachronism and probably, like the anti-Darwinian law in Arkansas, no great harm was going to be done by picking this up as a basis to write a judicial essay on, because this is one of the nicest ways a judge can find to perpetuate his philosophy for posterity. But, when I looked at the present status of abortion legislation—and until last year it was almost, for practical purposes, an unbroken wall of legislation calling most abortions criminal—I do not see an openly acknowledged acceptance of therapeutic abortions. I do not think that many judges are going to accept the idea that this criminal law of considerable antiquity, in terms of official pronouncements and uniform enforcement, is suddenly in violation of equal protection, vague, and indefinite. I don't expect this. It may be a long uphill climb.

But the constitutional theories advanced here probably will be used to amplify further the new legislation. For example, if I read this California statute right, a woman beyond twenty weeks of pregnancy would not under any circumstances be permitted to have an abortion, even though her life is in danger.

GAMPELL: That is what it seems to say.

GEORGE: It seems to me that this is the kind of case where the equal protection, the arbitrary classification idea, might be at hand. Here the legislature has acted. It has acted very recently. It tried to confer a benefit on a much broadened class of persons, but in doing so, it used an arbitrary test which leaves this person outside the pale, where indeed she might have been within the coverage under the older statute, and I would not expect the court, if it bought this argument, to void the new statute. I would expect it to void the limitation to twenty weeks' pregnancy. If it did now do that, in effect, by judicial action, you are pushing an already-expanded statutory coverage out a little bit further.

I would say that, while there are some attacks that could be made, the results would not be a restoration of the older statute, but a further augmentation of the new.

PILPEL: I would like to point out, with respect to the anticontraception laws, twenty-eight states did have restrictive laws on birth control. As far as abortion laws are concerned, you referred to their uniform enforcement, and I am sure you know that there has been, on the whole, uniform nonenforcement.

GEORGE: But there is uniform pronouncement. You say there are all these states with birth control legislation. Well, how broadly do you read *Griswold?* Because *Griswold* can be read for all kinds of things that a strict constructionist would say it doesn't stand for at all.

WHITE: I have known of a number of abortions which under the laws of Texas were clearly illegal, no question about it. Here's my question, and I address it to the panel collectively: If you were my attorney and I said, "Here is this lady, and I am going to advise a therapeutic abortion, and it does not in my mind fit under the law," what would you advise me to do?

My personal philosophy is that I feel that, if I act in good faith, thoughtfully consider the situation, get the counsel of a respected colleague and we are in agreement, I am perfectly willing to take my chances in the courts. I don't think I am in grave jeopardy, but if you are my attorney, what would you tell me to do?

GAMPELL: Your attorney must tell you that the proposed action is unlawful. But I nevertheless thought I would never see the day when a doctor was prosecuted for doing a hospital abortion. And now nine California doctors have been so charged.

OVERSTREET: But the nine San Francisco doctors had only administrative disciplinary action taken against them, not criminal prosecution.

GAMPELL: It is important to realize, no matter how sacrosanct the practice of medicine is, that the law does not recognize private lawmaking. That is what everybody was doing in California. The doctors were being very ethical and proper, but they were paying not even lip service to the California Penal Code.

It seems to me like an excellent idea, but no matter how right you feel or how much your colleagues push you on, they can push you right into the penitentiary.

PILPEL: I do not think that is a fair statement.

MEANS: May I also disagree with that. After all, the question of whether or not the doctor is violating the law depends on whether the law, as applied to that particular case, is constitutional, because there is a higher law of the Constitution.

Now, the Superior Court of San Francisco County has just held that the constitutional grounds given by Judge Eyman there under the Eighth Amendment did, in fact, carve out an exception to the seemingly boundless scope of Section 274 of the California Penal Code. If a doctor comes to a lawyer and asks, "Is what I am doing illegal?" you can't give him a simplistic answer by looking up the statute. You have to look at the Constitution.

WHITE: That was not the question I will ask my lawyer. I know it is illegal. And I will ask him, as my lawyer, "What do you advise me to do?"

SCHWARTZ: Before I would accept that from you, I would tell you my judgment as to whether it is legal or illegal. Tell me why you think you should perform the abortion and then I will decide.

WHITE: Let me be specific. Assume a nineteen-year-old, feeble-minded girl in a training program for feeble-minded people. She has an IQ of about 70, and she could just about survive as an independent human being if her training program goes on. She becomes pregnant.

SCHWARTZ: One of the things I would tell you, if the statute allows abortion to preserve her life, is that "I don't know. That is one of the problems with vagueness. I don't know how the courts would read it, but if you and your colleagues consider that she could not survive as an independent human being, and this is a good-faith judgment, and you could get other doctors to sustain you in this, then go ahead and try it." You might ultimately lose, but that is the problem with a vague statute.

GAMPELL: Where you mislead me, Dr. White, is by saying it is illegal. From the facts you gave, it is legal. Anybody with any perception would say, "Sign the thing and say that, in your opinion, it is necessary to save her life." That is the end of the controversy.

LEAVY: Most of us are in agreement that under these facts we would advise the doctor to go ahead, with certain safeguards. I disagree with Dr. Gampell's previous statement that a doctor is inviting prison. Physicians are not sent to prison nor even condemned by the criminal courts if they are acting in good faith and not passing money in the abortion racket. The *Shively* case in California involving rubella abortions is a fluke. It is the first of its kind in the United States, and was motivated principally by the climate in California surrounding the abortion question immediately before the legislature. This action by the State Board of Medical Examiners was started by people who held very strong views and pressured the Attorney General into doing something. And the Attorney General refused to go any further. In fact, he was asked if he would initiate a criminal prosecution and he wouldn't do it, since the doctors acted openly and in good faith.

PILPEL: Nor have the cases been lost yet.

LUCAS: I would stress the importance of documenting your reasons in this particular case for performing the abortion, in order to protect yourself. If the police or investigators should come there, for example, it would be good for you to have a substantial case history of this girl written up. Your files also should contain a letter from your attorney interpreting the law, and saying that the history indicates a danger to the girl's longevity, and a letter from a colleague saying the same thing. If and when an investigator comes into your office, your records will indicate nothing more than a proper ethical and legal termination of pregnancy. Chances are that there will be no proceedings against you.

PILPEL: Apart from constitutional arguments, if I were the lawyer for the physician in this situation I would say what I said this morning, namely, that the statute is not self-explanatory, that anything which adversely affects health affects life, and that the situation you described is one, I think, that does not fall within the purview of the statutory prohibition.

If, by some chance, the physician were prosecuted under these facts, I think most of the panel would say that, recognizing that we could not with certainty anticipate the final decision, either the physician would be found not guilty or the statute would be held unconstitutional, at least as it applied to the doctor.

WHITE: Let me give you briefly the other case. A thirty-two-year-old married woman with three fine children and a good moral background, and the like, who didn't want any more children, and her husband has a vasectomy. He was away for a few weeks and she went to a cocktail party, had a few too many martinis, and became pregnant by someone other than her husband.

GAMPELL: There is one way to analyze both of your cases. If you use enough semantic tricks there isn't any abortion problem, because there is no case which is not capable of being analyzed as being a threat to the life of the pregnant woman. But on the basis of the facts you gave, there aren't going to be many physicians who would abort her. Society's attitude today, at least through male eyes, is that she is a wicked woman who got pregnant out of wedlock, and, by God, it serves her right!

GRANFIELD: Speaking purely as a lawyer, and as one who has been teaching law students rather than as a judge dealing with lawyers, it amazes me when we consider Texas as a strict jurisdiction, which justifies abortion only to save the life of the woman, and poor Dr. White is trying to present a case of an illegal abortion, and he wants a panel of lawyers to tell him it is against the law, but he gets nothing but a green light!

GAMPELL: Not from me!

SCHWARTZ: That is not true.

GRANFIELD: He didn't get any red lights. He didn't get any advice that this is clearly wrong. I think you ought not to do that, and I am speaking as a lawyer now, not as a priest or moralist.

SCHWARTZ: I think there is a real question of what is right or wrong when you are dealing with statutes which are inherently vague to start with, especially in this period of great flux. I disagree with Professor George on the hope of what we can expect if a battery of cases bangs away often enough at the anti-abortion statutes. That New Jersey case was a four to three decision, and there are a number of other split decisions. If one keeps hacking away, there will be changes. It may not take too long a time judicially. You never can tell.

The public opinion polls are phenomenal in reporting the widespread support for abortion law reform. This thing is snowballing. The answer to the doctor's question is that there really isn't any firm answer. By one reading of the statute you may be commiting an illegal act. By another reading of the statute you are not. And at the moment nobody knows clearly what the answer is; my bet would be that you would get away with it without very much trouble, particularly if you go through the documentation that is required

GEORGE: Aren't you expecting more of the lawyer than you should?

WHITE: No. Not if I came to you with a clear-cut case.

GEORGE: Under the law of Texas I think we could tell you that if it were put to a judge he would have to say that at least your second case, if not both cases, would be illegal abortions. It is one thing to obtain opinions from your colleagues in order to justify medical treatment, but it is quite different in the context of a criminal case or disciplinary action. If you have the burden of getting your professional colleagues to come into court and join you in saying, "Yes, it is our considered medical judgment that this woman would have died," I believe you would have a tough case to defend.

And, therefore, if I would have to come into the courtroom context, I would be hard put to defend you; but the probabilities of your being moved against under these circumstances are minimal, as long as the woman stays alive and well, and you have followed the procedural safeguards previously recommended, and as long as somebody doesn't want to make a celebrated case out of this. So the statistical probabilities are slim that you will end up being the fall guy to test the Texas law. When I told you that, I think I would have discharged, for the moment, my responsibility as counsel.

It is now up to you as a physician whether to accept the conservative approach, or to say, "No, if it comes to a conflict between what my conscience tells me I should do for my patient, and what this archaic law tells me, I will go ahead with what I feel to be in the best interests of my patient, using sound medical judgment, and take the consequences as they come." And I don't think you can put that judgment, the burden of making that judgment, on your attorney.

PILPEL: The New Jersey Supreme Court has stood for the proposition which, in its own words, is as follows: "That abortion is permissible where a physician performs an abortion because of a good faith determination in accordance with accepted medical standards that an abortion is immediately indicated."

If that is the way that the laws are going to be interpreted, and I don't feel irresponsible in saying that I think they may well be, that may answer, to some extent, Dr. White's questions.

WHITE: My final question is: What kind of research data do you want from us as medical and social scientists, that would be of the greatest help to you? For example, the data presented by Dr. Montgomery about rubella seems to me to make such an open-and-shut case that no court in the land would give you a hard time. And you can show with this precision really what you are dealing with in terms of the malformation of the fetus.

We have a much vaguer situation in determining what the

mother's attitude of rejection does to an unwanted baby's development, but we do have some data to show very clearly that maternal rejection in certain instances can result in the failure of development of such primitive functions as speech, in reduction of the capacity to walk and to think clearly, and even can result in the death of the infant, not because it hasn't been fed or kept warm enough, but because it was not given the right kind of maternal stimulation and love.

Are there experiments we could do, or data that have already been collected that we could pull together and put at your disposal, that would help your position in going before the courts?

SCHWARTZ: This is important. I think in two areas we are going to need substantial bodies of proof to present to an appellate court, if not a lower court, and that is the question of what happens to an abortee who goes outside the law. There are perhaps one million women aborted every year in the United States. What happens to them? What do they go through? I think that Whittemore's study is very significant. We need something like that on a larger scale.

Secondly, we ought to know what happens to the unwanted child who is born because the woman is unable to terminate the pregnancy. The court is, I think, going to be particularly receptive to these sociological problems when you are talking about a million or more illegal abortions a year in this country. This is a problem which, if you can document it to a high court, can't be overlooked. It is something that doesn't belong in the law if this kind of destruction is going on. And women are denied medical care in all these cases.

WHITE: We can do two more studies, similar to that which Mr. Whittemore presented today, in other communities, and find essentially the same things. Would you feel this in itself would be a powerful weapon in your hands legally?

LEAVY: I believe so. The sociological problem is one of the greatest impacts that we can make upon a court at this time.

LUCAS: With reference to the question about what kind of data would be most useful, there are three particular things which I think would be extremely useful in preparing this broadside attack that we are working on in New York State. These are data which are not available yet, as far as I can tell, and which we will have to piece together from our own physicians in the state.

One would be to show the vagueness of the abortion statutes, to show that in your day-to-day practice, you can't interpret the statute because it is unclear. You don't know how to act when you have patients coming in.

The second would be to show that the existence of the statute, even in its vague form, seriously deters you from exercising your best medical judgment; that you turn patients away to the netherland of criminal abortions because you are afraid of being prosecuted, or you are afraid of public scorn or scorn from your colleagues.

And the third, which would be very difficult to come up with, would require a substantial building of public opinion. The best thing we could have would be a statistically valid opinion survey showing that 90 per cent of the physicians in your locale favor a freedom-of-choice plan. That would be extremely helpful, but it is not available yet.

PILPEL: There seems to be no question that the risk of maternal mortality and morbidity in childbirth goes up after a certain number of children. There is a genuine peril to life in cases where women already have a number of children. That is another kind of datum that I think we already have.

QUAY: Mr. Leavy's suggestion for investigations should include one which has been neglected, and which seems to me would be highly valuable: a follow-up study on the women who apply for abortion and are not granted relief. What happens to them? What mortality or morbidity results?

MRS. PILPEL: That is a good suggestion.

ABORTION AND PROGENY

The Role of Abortion in Preventing Congenital Derangement and Emotional Deprivation

Leon Eisenberg, M.D. (moderator)
Kenneth R. Niswander, M.D. (rapporteur)
Kurt Hirschhorn, M.D.
John R. Montgomery, M.D.
William B. Ober, M.D.
Philip M. Sarrel, M.D.

L. Eisenberg: We are concerned with the genetic, biological, and other factors that may lead to a defective fetus, as well as with the consequences of being born unwanted. The management of unwanted pregnancies and the mothers and children involved is another area of our interest. The first speaker on our panel is Dr. Kurt Hirschhorn.

Hirschhorn: I am going to discuss the genetic indications for abortion. Some of these recent advances in prenatal diagnosis, however, have very little to do with the main subject of this meeting, which is the unwanted pregnancy.

When a couple wants a child and the fetus happens to carry gene or chromosome aberrations which will make the child abnormal, an abortion is often considered. It is hoped that with the newer techniques that are available a family can have a normal child at a later time. This situation, of course, accounts for a small minority of the abortions that are being performed or will ever probably be performed. Also, I feel that this genetic indication should not even be included in the arguments that are presented before legislatures. If we are going to have abortion laws at all, there should be a separate law that pertains to families who must choose whether to have a child with a familial genetic deficiency. I think it is important to stress this distinction.

Recent improvements in tissue culture techniques have made it possible to grow cells derived from amniotic fluid obtained from amniocentesis between the twelfth and sixteenth week of pregnancy. These cells can be demonstrated to be of fetal origin and their genetic makeup, therefore, reflects the genetic makeup of the fetus. Based on several thousand amniocenteses in this country, this procedure in the early months of pregnancy appears to be harmless both to the mother and to the fetus.

The fluid and the cells that are obtained can be examined by several techniques with different aims in mind. The fluid itself, for example, can be studied for enzyme content or for accumulation of certain metabolites that the fetus excretes. In this way we are able to detect certain inborn errors of metabolism. To cite one example, the absence of alpha glucosidase in the amniotic fluid of a multigravida who has had a previously affected child indicates that the child is going to be affected by a genetic disease which will make him quite sick for the few years that he lives.

Another example might be informative. An accumulation of uric acid in the amniotic fluid is good presumptive evidence, with the proper genetic background in the family, that the child will be affected by a syndrome consisting of mental retardation and a self-mutilation urge which will cause him to rip at himself for the rest of his life.

One can apply to the amniotic fluid cells a simple nuclear stain which will indicate quite readily what the sex of the fetus is. Sex is important in diseases which are inherited in a sex-linked manner, such as hemophilia, in which, as you know, the female is a carrier and transmits the disease to the male. In this case a female child will be normal. A male child, on the other hand, runs a 50 per cent risk of being affected with hemophilia.

These cells can also be examined directly for enzyme content, or more commonly the cells can be put into tissue culture and grown until they form a large layer, and this huge population of cells can be examined for their enzyme content. In tissue culture, in fact, one can detect at least twenty different forms of inborn errors of metabolism by means of enzyme defects in these cultures. Some ten of these have now been diagnosed in affected fetuses.

L. EISENBERG: I didn't quite understand. Ten different kinds of disorders have in fact been diagnosed?

HIRSCHHORN: Yes, these have actually been diagnosed in affected fetuses.

L. EISENBERG: There are a large number of potentially diagnosable cases, which have not yet been diagnosed because the opportunity has not presented itself?

HIRSCHHORN: That's right. We do know that in all cases where the opportunity has presented itself the amnion cells have behaved like every other cell in tissue culture.

Another approach to genetic diagnosis is to grow amniotic fluid cells and inspect their chromosomes. There are, as you know, individuals who carry certain chromosome defects, namely translocations, who have a very high risk of producing children who are chromosomally abnormal. The most common defect of this type is mongolism.

Usually in mongolism there are three No. 21 chromosomes instead of the normal pair and a total chromosome number of 47. Occasionally, however, the extra No. 21 is attached to another chromosome. If one investigates the mother, or occasionally the father, of such a mongoloid child, one finds that the mother has one free 21 and has her second one attached to another chromosome. Such a mother, by statistics from known families, has about a one in five chance of having a mongoloid child. Analysis of cells derived from the amniotic fluid of such carrier mothers will reveal in fact whether or not the fetus will be mongoloid. If so, appropriate action can be taken. The time that is required for these studies is short enough so that a definitive answer can be obtained by the fifth month and frequently the fourth month of pregnancy. The rate of success of actual tissue culture of these cells among those laboratories performing amniocenteses is about 70 per cent on the first attempt. This technique can be repeated without harm, and has been done a number of times on a single patient by several investigators.

Now, what is the advantage of utilizing amniotic fluid diagnosis rather than using conventional genetic counseling? We can now go to the prospective parents and, in addition to telling them that they have a three out of four chance of having a normal child, we can tell them with certainty which three will be normal. The fourth can be aborted if they so desire. This is quite a different kind of genetic counseling—with a guarantee of normal offspring.

L. Eisenberg: Do you have to wait until the twelfth to sixteenth week because of the difficulty of obtaining amniotic fluid before then?

Hirschhorn: Yes. The twelfth week of actual pregnancy, that is the fourteenth week after the last menstrual period, seems to be the earliest that you can do it.

L. Eisenberg: Do you do it vaginally?

Hirschhorn: The vaginal approach carries with it the danger of infection. There has never to my knowledge been an infection from the abdominal approach.

Alexaniants: Have you ever experienced complications after this?

Hirschhorn: Not with early amniocentesis. This early form of amniocentesis has now been done in at least 2,000 cases. Of course, second- and third-trimester amniocentesis has been done on many thousands for the Rh factor.

Of the 2,000 done so far, of which the vast majority have been permitted to go to term, I know of no case of damage to the fetus. The reason for this safety is that the fetus is extremely free-floating at that particular time and able to avoid the needle by moving out of your way if you touch it.

L. Eisenberg: Dr. Sarrel will now share with us some of his experiences in running a clinic for unmarried pregnant high-school students who previously had been excluded from high school and condemned to a life of repeated unwanted pregnancies and social inutility. There have been a few pioneering clinics, of which the one at Yale has been the most successful, and Dr. Sarrel will give us a brief resumé of what these experiences have been.

SARREL: My subject is the problem of pregnancy in poverty-bound, unwed teenagers and the role of abortion in their lives. Both the individual's health and the whole structure of her family life is affected by the pregnancy. The increasing numbers of venereal disease patients and of teen-age unwed mothers in this country testify to the lack of knowledge on the part of the teen-age population. Indeed very little has been done for the teen-age population to prepare them for their sexual roles. Sex education in this country is in a very early stage. Contraceptives are not available to most teen-agers. Abortion, legal and illegal, is also rare in the teen-age girl who becomes pregnant out of wedlock before the age of twenty.

In some urban ghettos the illegitimacy rate is as high as 50 per cent. When one considers the number of girls who don't get pregnant, one can estimate that at least the majority in this population have premarital intercourse. At the same time, however, family-life education programs are almost unknown in the ghetto. Pregnant unwed teenagers in the poverty group have little choice but to leave school, have their babies, keep them, and become part of a subculture within the poverty group, the one-parent family.

All too often in this group the initial pregnancy leads to a destructive cycle consisting of failure to finish education, pregnancy complicated by obstetrical disease, dependence on welfare, and recidivism. A 5-year follow-up study on 100 teen-age unwed mothers, age 17 or younger, who delivered a baby out of wedlock in New Haven in 1959 and 1960 showed that at the end of 5 years, 95 per cent had had repeat pregnancies. Ninety-one per cent were still unmarried, 60 per cent were supported by welfare, and a total of 249 repeat pregnancies were conceived. Of the five girls who did not have a repeat pregnancy, one had contacted gonorrhea and was sterile. Another was in a mental hospital and a third was an alcoholic with cirrhosis.

Abortion was not a significant factor in coping with these pregnancies. Our studies concur with Robert Hall's in documenting the nonavailability of legal abortion for this group. There was one therapeutic abortion in the total of 349 pregnancies, despite the fact that a number of the girls were between 12 and 15 years old. In addition, very few criminal abortionists would undertake to do an abortion for a minor in New Haven who had no financial resources. In our study of the total 349 pregnancies, only 9 abortions were documented, and, of these, only 2 were septic. They occurred among the 9 women who were married and who might have some possibility of obtaining funds for an abortionist. Adoption, similarly, was not available. Eighty-four per cent of the girls were Negro. Two of their babies were adopted. Although it is true that many Negro girls have no desire to give a baby for adoption, it is also true that it is almost impossible to find couples to adopt Negro babies. In Connecticut, approximately 55 per cent of the Caucasian babies born out of wedlock are adopted, while less than 5 per cent of the Negro babies are adopted. The result is the development of a family guided by a poorly educated, immature, dependent mother who manages a minimal adjustment to the strains of everyday life. One does not need too much imagination to see the effect of such a family life upon the progeny.

Our approach in New Haven since 1965 has been multidisciplinary care—social work, medical care, education, vocational training—for both the pregnant teen-age girl and her family. Building upon the doctor-patient relationship and other professional-client relationships, we have used the pregnancy as a vehicle for family-life education, continuation of formal education, and, most importantly, building of self-esteem and establishment of new roles—maternal, educational, and vocational.

The results have been promising. Complications of pregnancy such as toxemia and prematurity have been almost eliminated. Over 95 per cent of the patients have returned to school following delivery. The number of girls with repeat pregnancies has been minimal, less than 10 per cent. Perhaps most significant is that among our first 231 patients (98 per cent of whom were Negro), all but 2 kept their babies and 22 have gone on to a college education. Two therapeutic abortions have been done, under the Connecticut law, on repeat pregnancies. The remainder of the 16 girls with repeat pregnancies have not desired interruption of the pregnancy. I might add that 10 of the 16 were married.

Pregnancy in the unwed, poverty-bound teen-ager poses such a tremendous threat to the well-being of mother and child that it is not unreasonable to consider it life-threatening. Therapeutic abortion should be made available for such a youngster. If abortion were offered within the same kind of multidisciplinary framework that we have utilized in treating out-of-wedlock pregnancy, perhaps similar results could be obtained while preventing the immature girl from being subjected to the medical, social, and psychic trauma of continuing a pregnancy. At the same time, one would prevent the birth of a child whose potential is so drastically limited by the milieu in which he would have to be brought up. Certainly, there is an important place for legal abortion in this fight against deprivation.

L. EISENBERG: One question. Did I understand you to say 22 of the 231 girls have gone to college?

SARREL: Yes. Almost all with full scholarships.

L. EISENBERG: That must be a much higher rate than for the general population out of the areas from which they come.

SARREL: These are all Negro girls who had a baby out of wedlock and kept it.

L. EISENBERG: So this is better than they would have done if they had been Negro males or Negro females without being pregnant coming from more affluent areas.

SARREL: Yes. In fact, there is some criticism because a girl is better off if she gets pregnant and enters our program.

L. EISENBERG: Dr. Montgomery will present some data on fetal risk related to infection.

MONTGOMERY: In order properly to evaluate the role of abortion in preventing congenital derangement, I think we should spend a minute reviewing rubella as the prototype of the causes of congenital anomalies produced as the result of insults to the fetus during pregnancy. These insults may, of course, be due to many factors other than infection.

It has been estimated that 20,000 to 30,000 infants were affected by the 1963 to 1965 epidemic. The mortality rate from congenital rubella is approximately 30 per cent. From these estimates, there are between 14,000 and 21,000 survivors in the United States. These figures are only estimates and they are probably too low.

By January 1965, a large enough group of these infants had been diagnosed in the Houston area to justify setting up a special rubella follow-up clinic at the Texas Children's Hospital, sponsored by private and public funds, primarily the Children's Bureau. From this study and others, the original syndrome described by Gregg, namely congenital eye defects, heart disease, deafness, and mental retardation, was expanded to include a much larger number of findings. These findings included purpura, thrombocytopenia, anemia, enlarged liver and spleen, jaundice, pneumonia, encephalitis, bone lesions, skin manifestations, diarrhea, kidney abnormalities, growth retardation, immunologic abnormalities, and other anomalies.

Out of the first 100 children cared for in this clinic, 20 died and 16 were lost to follow-up, leaving 64 patients. The findings in these 64 patients were as follows:

Bilateral cataracts	18 patients
Unilateral cataracts	19 patients
Glaucoma	1 patient
Chorioretinitis	20 patients
Hearing loss (definite)	45 patients
Poor speech	27 patients

In addition, 69 of the 100 children had congenital heart lesions.

As the survivors grew older the problems changed from those of an acute illness to those of a chronic handicapping disease, and developmental abnormalities became apparent.

Excellent cooperation was obtained from our community. The Houston Speech and Hearing Center, the Cerebral Palsy Treatment Center, the Lighthouse for the Blind, the Council for Retarded Children, and the Child and Family Service Center provided special services in their fields of competence. In many cases a child attended sessions in two or more of these institutions.

In the spring of 1967, 69 children who were two and a half years of age were examined by a multidisciplined medical group. Twenty children were classified as multihandicapped. Although no two children in the multihandicapped group were exactly alike, the combination of lesions most frequently seen was visual defects due to cataracts or glaucqma, hearing loss due to neurosensory impairment, and neuromuscular problems ranging from delayed motor development to frank cerebral palsy. Many also had congenital heart disease.

I think it is apparent from this presentation that the effects of rubella on the fetus can be devastating. The resulting problems for the family, the patient, and the community are enormous.

Laboratory tests are now available to prove the diagnosis of maternal rubella. When maternal rubella is proved during the early months of pregnancy substantial risk exists that the fetus will be affected. At the present time, abortion offers the only method of avoiding this risk.

L. EISENBERG: Has any effort been made with amniocentesis to grow the virus?

HIRSCHHORN: Amnion cells have been derived from abortion material and the amnion has been shown to be infected. Nobody to my knowledge has actually done this with amniocentesis.

MONTGOMERY: It is an obvious next step, and in the biology department we have grown the virus from the products of legal and illegal abortions and have been able to isolate the virus in nine out of ten products of conception studied.

L. EISENBERG: Our next statement will be by Dr. Niswander.

NISWANDER: I would like to describe the reaction of the medical profession in this country to the discovery that first-trimester rubella is teratogenic as an example of what *can* happen when the profession sees a human need. Obstetricians were early leaders in making abortions available to these gravidas. In spite of the cloudy legal status of aborting for pregnancy rubella, hundreds and possibly thousands of obstetricians have been willing to discuss with their patients the pros and cons of continuing a pregnancy complicated by first-trimester rubella, and indeed to interrupt the pregnancy if the patient and her husband chose not to incur the risk of fetal malformation.

Often the diagnosis of first-trimester rubella is a sufficient indication for therapeutic abortion. Occasionally the legally more comfortable, but clearly less precise, preoperative diagnosis of suicidal potential due to depression related to the likelihood of rubella-induced fetal malformation, is used. Governor Reagan did nothing to dispel the doctors' doubts on the legality of rubella abortions when he insisted that potential fetal malformation as an indication for abortion be deleted from the 1967 California Abortion Bill, later the California law.

Legislative approval of rubella abortions has been slow to arrive in other states also. The courts, however, are currently considering and, I hope, clarifying the issue. In California, the reprimand by the Board of Medical Examiners of two prominent San Francisco obstetricians for rubella abortions was overruled by the court. The decision is currently under appeal to a higher court. This action by the Board of Medical Examiners practically stopped hospital abortions for any reason in California for a time.

In a second important court case, a New York jury recently found a hospital guilty of negligence when it refused to abort a gravida for early rubella and for reassuring her of the harmlessness of the disease. The child born of the pregnancy has multiple major defects. This decision will be appealed. A court clarification of the rights of the patient and the doctor in this regard can be expected, at least in New York State. It is to be hoped that ultimately the constitutionality of the state abortion laws will be considered by the United States Supreme Court.

I have discussed at perhaps too great length the rubella controversy and how obstetricians have reacted to it, because the resolution of this problem must precede any substantial increase in the number of abortions done for major fetal disease.

It should be remembered that an estimated 30,000 children with major defects were born in the United States as a result of the 1964 rubella epidemic in spite of the fact that many, probably thousands, of rubella abortions were performed in the United States that year.

Although some of these abnormal children probably resulted from unrecognized mild maternal disease, undoubtedly many of the gravidas not aborted either sought abortion and were refused, or were not aware of the potential hazards of the disease, or could simply not make a proper medical connection. With clarification of the law, liberal obstetricians will make abortion more widely available to patients who, because of rubella or some other reason, run a substantial risk of bearing an abnormal child. A tragedy such as that which occurred in 1964 must not be allowed to happen again in spite of the questionable legality of abortion in this instance.

L. EISENBERG: Our final panelist is Dr. Ober.

OBER: I would like to offer you some sporadic observations which a few of my colleagues and I have made in a rather unsystematic fashion over the past decade. My observations are based upon autopsies of spontaneously aborted fetuses in the 400- and 500-gram range, up to 1,600 and even 1,800 grams. This is an area in pathology which is not very well explored.

We have found that there is evidence of transplacental transmission of infectious diseases in a wide variety of conditions which we cannot define. We have very little or very feeble evidence of what was wrong with the mother prior to the abortion.

There are a few positive things that can be identified quite readily. I have seen inclusion disease fairly widely distributed in the tissues of two or three fetuses in the range of approximately 1,000 to 1,500 grams. This infection produces spontaneous abortion or death in the uterus. A friend of mine has told me of a case of fetal herpes with a clear history of herpes simplex infection of the mother.

It is not uncommon to find a nonspecific pneumonitis when bacterial stains are done upon sections of the lung. We do not discover visible bacteria and we do not recover fungi, and the inference is presumably that whatever infection was present may well have been viral. However, when we go back into the mother's history we do not get much in the way of positive information. Usually, the infection was a mild one or incidental or subclinical. I have seen a number of severe cardiac malformations in children who, if the pregnancy had continued, would have had the syndrome of polyhydramnios. We have also seen rather severe intracranial lesions with extensive malformation of the brain. Unfortunately, when you add all these up and try to make scientific sense out of them in terms suitable for publication, you cannot succeed because the material is inconsistent and sporadically detected. I would like to suggest that this is an area of pathological anatomy which needs to be explored, and it is an area which can yield very fruitful results.

L. EISENBERG: We have one final communication from the panel, the briefest statement of the conference. Dr. Virginia Apgar, Vice President for Medical Affairs of the National Foundation, has sent this telegram: "From human studies only, the drugs known to produce abnormalities of the fetus are aminopterin, thalidomide, and progesterone. State of contraceptives equivocal. Many drugs, such as aspirin and caffeine, cause chromosome breaks. No evidence of genetic damage. Eggs and sperm should be protected from radiation exposure whenever possible."

Now I think we might call on members of the audience to share their thoughts and experiences and address questions to us. I wonder whether our visitors from abroad would comment on the situation in their own countries. What is the accepted medical method of treating suspected fetal abnormalities?

ALEXANIANTS: The main medical diagnoses are the same everywhere. In the Soviet Union we have very few problems because we can interrupt pregnancies whenever there is a need, without any legal complications. Where there is any suspicion that some abnormality may occur in the fetus, the obstetrician will consult with a specialist and a decision based on the best solution for the mother is made. Any other solution would be considered punishment for the parents and for society, and bad economically.

L. EISENBERG: Dr. Engström, what is the situation in Sweden?

ENGSTROM: After the thalidomide tragedy, a new indication for legal abortion was included in the Swedish law. According to that indication, every woman who has contracted rubella before the fourteenth or fifteenth week of pregnancy (or thinks she had rubella) can have a legal abortion, and she is informed about this by the physician. I am interested by what Dr. Hirschhorn pointed out—the importance of helping mothers who really want children.

MONTGOMERY: While we have our foreign guests available, could I ask one other question? Do you have trouble in your country with physicians who give gamma globulin before the serologic diagnosis of rubella is made?

ENGSTRÖM: Yes, since gamma globulin is free of charge for pregnant women, many obtain it. The question is, might she have suffered a subclinical infection in spite of the gamma globulin?

L. EISENBERG: I have the impression that even after gamma globulin there is still a considerable fetal risk, perhaps somewhat less, but still significant.

SARREL: I think we can quote the work of Dorothy Horstmann at Yale in which she has shown that gamma globulin does not prevent the viremia. We prefer not to give gamma globulin to our patients who are exposed, and if they develop any signs of the disease then we perform therapeutic abortion.

NISWANDER: It is worth pointing out, too, that we have felt secure in the belief that rubella occurring later than twelve or thirteen weeks' gestation is not teratogenic. Janet Hardy from Johns Hopkins has shown quite clearly that there is considerable fetal hazard to rubella in the midtrimester. A different congenital syndrome results, but one quite as damaging.

L. EISENBERG: May I interrupt as chairman to give some time to other considerations and other functions of this panel. If one is concerned with the issue of illegal abortion, the real problem in the United States, as Dr. Hirschhorn has pointed out, will not be solved at all by any of the so-called liberalized laws. The question is: Do the parents want the child or not? A child presumably normal physically, born of a mother who never wanted to have him, perhaps tried to abort him, or did not want him at this time, starts life in a precarious social setting. Everyone of us has seen children who were conceived unintentionally, where the mother apparently became reconciled to the pregnancy before term, and who seemed to have shown the same normal love and affection for that child as she did for others. One sees other cases where the mother never does quite get over her rejection of the child. We have no assurance, however, that she will not be able to be an adequate mother toward him. Any substantial body of data on this question is simply not available.

I would like to suggest that it is absurd for us to consider rubella or the few medical complications of pregnancy or the question of possible psychiatric hazards to either mother or child as the only justifications for abortion on reasonable request of the mother. Rather, abortion is a question of the rights of mothers and of human dignity and happiness. Physicians should not become so involved with medical issues that basic human rights are ignored.

Mrs. Beck, you had a conference at the Children's Bureau on the unwanted-child question. Would you say something to the group about that?

BECK: The conference was sponsored by the National Institute of Mental Health and the National Institute of Child Health, with the Children's Bureau.

That conference had a somewhat different focus. We were primarily concerned with identifying the high-priority researchable areas in the field of abortion as a major public health problem with respect to the unwanted child. Information on the quality of life to which the child is very often condemned is scanty. We are curious, for example, to know something about the social adjustment of the unwanted child who ends up in an institutional program and remains in institutional care throughout childhood. It seems very important to us to examine the quality of life of these children. This is a very high-priority problem that does concern us, and we will welcome information about studies if anybody has conducted them, and we will be very pleased to talk with investigators who are interested in undertaking projects of this type.

HIRSCHHORN: Are there any other comments?

OBER: Dr. Sarrel has defined a very high-risk population, and possibly he could shed some light on what happens to the children born to these teen-age mothers who are unmarried and who come from a very low socioeconomic population.

SARREL: There is a real social problem developing in this group when the first pregnancy is followed by others and becomes a way of life. For the majority this does not happen. Our follow-up indicates that less than 15 per cent of the girls and their families are on welfare three years later, compared to 60 per cent in the previous group. If we were to compare our results with the 1959 to 1960 study, we would have had 180 children on welfare by now from just the first 100 girls in our group.

L. EISENBERG: Substantial information is being accumulated to suggest that brain development is very much dependent upon caloric intake, not only during pregnancy, but also during the first year of life. The studies that were reported at the International Conference on Nutrition indicated a rather direct relationship between cranial size and the transilluminability of the head and the mother's dietary history in a country where protein intake is rather low. Furthermore, a pediatrician at Cornell suggested that among severely malnourished infants there may be as much as 40 per cent reduction in the total number of cells within the brain, as determined by DNA content as a measure of the number of cells.

Frequently superimposed on these hazards is a cultural environment in which books are rarely available and the parents are relatively uneducated and have a much more limited language facility than that of the standard population. In addition, the school system makes no special effort to accommodate culturally deprived youngsters.

Then you have the questions of self-concept and the sense of inadequacy that is a result of segregation, of being born poor in a country with a marked class structure. The question of being unwanted is a separate kind of question. Many mothers would want children if they had the means to support them. The structure of support for families in this country is punitive and moralistic. The welfare system systematically degrades people in this country and almost assures that they will remain in the status that they are in.

ALEXANIANTS: Unwanted children are not a problem in my country, because we can have abortion on demand, but I would like to discuss what happens to the children who do not have fathers. I think, first of all, that it will be necessary to create a feeling in the community that this mother should not be condemned or considered a sinner. She should have understanding and acceptance in the community. It will help her to raise her child because there are some mothers who prefer not to be married but have children and raise them alone. The community must provide some material support for her to raise this child. Secondly, it must establish day-care centers for smaller children and boarding schools for older children to permit the mother to work. Such encouragement by society helps mothers to raise good, healthy children.

L. EISENBERG: Is there a different attitude toward the unmarried mother in the Rumanian Republic, for example, compared to the Georgian or the Russian areas? Are there cultural differences?

ALEXANIANTS: No, but there are very few unmarried mothers. For the few we have, there are lawyers in the outpatient department of the maternity home to help them solve their problems regarding work, housing, and the like.

OBER: As a nonpsychiatrist, I would like to ask Dr. Eisenberg a question. Given the situation of a child who is born to an unwed mother and is raised without a father, what psychodynamic deviations would be most likely to occur?

L. EISENBERG: My answer to the question, Dr. Ober, would be that it would depend on many variables: adequacy of housing, adequacy of schools, availability of work for the mother, and the existence of any male relatives or big brother services to help establish a male image for the child. Negro experience in the United States provides, I think, a rather clear demonstration that boys can grow up to be quite male in the absence of any constant father, despite psychiatric statements to the contrary. Support for young out-of-wedlock black girls comes much more readily from the other members of the black community than does white support for a middle-class white girl with an unwanted pregnancy. One sees large numbers of black children raised in foster homes where the foster parents would in every way qualify as adoptive parents if the state were prepared to give them a subsidy. They don't qualify for adoption because they don't have the money. The real basis for the difference in black and white adoption rates is the difference in the resources of the families that would be capable of adopting. So I feel that a child can grow up to be perfectly normal without a father, though I am much in favor of fathers.

In closing I think that we all agree that we should utilize presently available scientific information to approach the idea of a wanted healthy child with every pregnancy.

The day will come when society will have to deal with the individual's right to have an unreasonable number of children. The most democratic proposal for population control comes from a biologist who hopes that there will be a day when an antifertility agent will reduce fertility by 15 or 20 per cent. One could then put it in the drinking water and obtain a kind of Russian roulette. In that way, everybody would have a reduced chance of having children, and the net birth rate would drop to the optimum for the country. I hope that we can find a happier means of population control.

ABORTION AND WOMANKIND

Abortion as an Inherent Right,
an Occasional Prerogative,
or a Special Privilege

Mary Calderone, M.D. (moderator)
Sophia J. Kleegman, M.D. (rapporteur)
Barbara Dohrenwend, Ph.D.
Vera Houghton
Ruth W. Lidz, M.D.
Ruth Roemer, LL.B.
Alice S. Rossi, Ph.D.
Natalie Shainess, M.D.

CALDERONE: I now declare this meeting open, and remind you that Dr. Robert Hall deliberately made this a panel of women so that we would approach the question as women.

I will call on Dr. Dohrenwend first.

DOHRENWEND: I am reporting on a study designed to find out whether it is possible to determine the rate of illegal abortions in the United States. Serious doubts have arisen as to whether it is feasible to learn the true incidence of abortion in the United States. These doubts are based in part on the fact that previous attempts to interview systematically drawn samples of the adult female population have yielded rates as low as 1 per cent of women reporting ever having induced or attempted to induce an abortion.

The exception to this failure to get women to report induced abortions is the work of the Kinsey group. Of the married women they interviewed, about 22 per cent reported at least one abortion. However, because this sample was not systematically drawn from the adult female population of the United States, this finding has been considered to provide only a bit more evidence on which to base a guess as to the true rate in the population. It did, however, at least open the possibility that, if questions about abortions were asked in the right way, women might answer them honestly.

Specifically, I will report on the results of an experiment in which four interviewing techniques were used to survey systematic samples of women in a community in order to determine (1) whether it is possible to get more than about 1 per cent to report induced abortions, and (2) if so, what form of interview is most effective.

The interview schedules were varied in two ways. The first variation grew directly out of the innovative work of the Kinsey group. A number of critics have suggested that they may have obtained spuriously high rates for various types of "illicit" activity because they used directive questions which premised participation in these activities, usually in the form, "When did you first. . . ?" On the other hand, Kinsey and his colleagues argued that formulation of questions in this fashion served to overcome the tendency of respondents to deny such illicit activities, and did not lead to false admissions. To test the effect of this directive-interviewing tactic, therefore, we asked about induced abortions in two ways. In the nondirective version we asked questions in the form, "Did you ever have an abortion or do anything to stop a pregnancy?" And in the directive version in the form, "When did you have your first abortion or do something to stop a pregnancy?" Questions about abortion were asked, with different wordings, at several points in each interview schedule.

The second variation in interviewing technique involved the context in which the abortion questions were asked. In one type of interview, questions concerning the woman's reproductive history led up to the abortion questions. In the other variation, the abortion questions were preceded by questions focused on the woman's attitudes toward and knowledge about contraception and abortion.

In order to create a consistently nondirective or directive tone to the interview, the preceding contextual questions were written in the nondirective form when they were to be followed by nondirective abortion questions and, insofar as possible, in the directive form when they were to be followed by directive abortion questions.

The group of women interviewed was a subsample of a previously interviewed systematic sample of a section of New York City. To maximize the period during which they had been at risk of abortion and to minimize the chance of their having forgotten details about their abortions, we chose a subsample of women ranging in age from 35 through 49. All women in this age range were included, regardless of marital status. All of the interviewers were experienced and specially trained.

Table 1 shows the proportions of women who reported induced abortions for themselves, in the community sample as a whole, and on each of the four interview schedules. Clearly, these rates are much higher than the rates on the order of 1 per cent previously reported from interview studies of systematic community samples.

The question of which interview schedule is most effective is not so clearly answered by these data. However, the difference between the schedule yielding the highest rate, the Directive Attitude schedule, and the other three combined, would occur by chance less than 10 per cent of the time.

Given the finding that the highest rate was obtained from women reporting their own abortion experience on the Directive Attitude schedule, let us see how and why this approach was relatively effective. First, did it work equally well with all subgroups in the sample? Table 2 compares the responses of women with different educational and religious backgrounds, and shows that the Directive

Table 1   Proportion of Respondents in Community Sample Reporting One or More Induced Abortions for Themselves or for Friends According to Interview Schedule

| | Interview Schedule | | | | *All* |
	Nondirective History	*Directive History*	*Nondirective Attitude*	*Directive Attitude*	*Interview Schedules*
Per cent of respondents reporting one or more abortions for themselves	12.5	10.8	15.1	23.9[a]	15.5
Number of respondents	56	65	53	46	220
Per cent of friends reported as having had abortion	Not asked on these schedules		11.7	20.2	15.5
Number of friends			120[b]	99[b]	

[a]Chi square for the comparison of the four interview schedules is 4.1, df = 3, p = .25; chi square for the comparison of the Directive Attitude interview with the other three pooled is 3.6, df = 1, p < .10.

[b]The question concerning 3 friends or relatives was added to the schedules after 49 community interviews had been completed; for this reason it was asked on only 40 Nondirective and 33 Directive Attitude interviews.

Attitude schedule was highly effective with better-educated respondents, but not with less-educated respondents. In contrast to education, religion made little difference in responses to the Nondirective and Directive Attitude schedules.

Our second question about the Directive Attitude schedule is *why* it worked relatively well. The form, nondirective or directive, of the abortion questions seems to have been relatively unimportant since, as shown in Table 1, the lowest rate of abortions, by a small margin, was reported on the Directive History schedule. Furthermore, on three of the four schedules, the majority of respondents reported their abortions the first time they were asked, suggesting that it was important for the contextual questions to precede the first abortion question in determining the outcome of the interview.

The concept underlying the use of directive contextual questions preceding the abortion questions was that these questions might lead respondents to be more frank about their attitudes and knowledge concerning contraception and that this frankness would then carry

Table 2 Proportion of Respondents Reporting One or More Induced Abortions According to Interview Schedule and Respondent's Education and Religion (base for per cent in parentheses; cases with no answer on education or religion subtracted from base)

	Interview Schedule			
Respondent Education	*Nondirective History*	*Directive History*	*Nondirective Attitude*	*Directive Attitude*
Less than high school	11.1	3.7	21.7	15.0
graduate	(27)	(27)	(23)	(20)
High school graduate	14.3	15.8	10.0	30.8[a]
or better	(28)	(38)	(30)	(26)
Respondent Religion				
Roman Catholic	10.0	6.2	13.0	17.6
	(20)	(32)	(23)	(17)
Non-Roman Catholic	14.3	15.2	16.7	27.6
or none	(35)	(33)	(30)	(29)

[a]Comparison of rates on Nondirective versus Directive Attitude schedules for high school graduates yields a chi square of 3.8; df = 1; p = .05.

over to the abortion questions. The possibility of such a carry-over effect on the Directive Attitude schedule is suggested by the finding, shown in Table 3, that the proportion of respondents reporting knowledge, whether correct or incorrect, of how abortions are done, and the proportion reporting that one or more friends or relatives had had an abortion, was significantly higher on the Directive than on the Nondirective Attitude schedule. Moreover, this increase is almost entirely due to the better-educated respondents, suggesting a reason for their greater responsiveness to the Directive-Attitude schedule—i.e. it appears that, having responded to the directive questions by showing themselves to be generally knowledgeable concerning abortions, they were then less reluctant to report their personal abortion experience.

One important issue raised by these results that cannot be resolved

Table 3 Proportions of Respondents Reporting Knowledge of How Abortions Are Done or that at Least One of Three Friends Had an Abortion, According to Interview Schedule and Respondent Education (base for per cent in parentheses; cases with no answer subtracted from base)

Type of Interview Schedule	Respondent Education	
	Less than High School Graduate	*High School Graduate or Better*
	Per Cent Reporting Knowledge of How Abortions Are Done	
Nondirective Attitude	34.8	37.8
	(23)	(29)
Directive Attitude	36.8	76.9
	(19)	(26)
	$\chi^2 = 0.02$; df = 1; p $>$ .05	$\chi^2 = 8.47$; df = 1; p $<$ .05
	Per Cent Reporting at Least One or More Friends Known to Have Had Abortion	
Nondirective Attitude	34.8	17.9
	(23)	(28)
Directive Attitude	47.4	53.8
	(19)	(26)
	$\chi^2 = 0.68$; df = 1; p $>$ .05	$\chi^2 = 7.66$; df = 1; p $<$ .05

by this study is whether the less-educated respondents gave fairly complete reports on both forms or, alternatively, underreported on both nondirective and directive interviews. The latter seems more likely if we reason that, because the directive knowledge questions did not elicit more positive responses than the nondirective questions from these respondents, no catalyst was present to facilitate frankness on the directive abortion questions. Perhaps, therefore, we should next search for a type of attitude or knowledge on which directive questions will influence the responses of less-educated women to see whether the catalytic effect will work with them, as it appears to have worked with better-educated women, that is, to persuade them to provide a relatively accurate report of their experiences with induced abortions.

SHAINESS: Did you provide assurance of confidence?

DOHRENWEND: A letter was sent to each woman saying that this was to be a study of her health, but not saying that we intended to ask her about abortion. When the interview started, she was reassured about anonymity and told that we considered this to be very important and needed information.

ROSSI: Was the letter sent on a letterhead?

DOHRENWEND: Yes, of the School of Public Health.

ROSSI: Do you think that played a role?

DOHRENWEND: That is something that I have not tested. It might have.

CALDERONE Were there any differences in the level of education of the refusers?

DOHRENWEND: I don't think so.

DENNISTON: Did you consider using women of the same socioeconomic backgrounds?

DOHRENWEND: We matched race for race. As far as socioeconomic background, in one sense one never matches because the role of interviewer is middle-class. This is sometimes highly important, since most of these were high school girls, with maybe a few in college. Say that they fell into a vague middle-class.

FLECK: Was illegal abortion considered or is this assumed?

DOHRENWEND: Actually I was not primarily interested in the legality of these abortions. The great majority were illegal. There were a few that were borderline, done in a hospital, but not necessarily legal.

DENNISTON: What extrapolation can you make in terms of race?

DOHRENWEND: The interesting thing here is that in the United States population, I don't have the slightest idea how this relates.

HOUGHTON: In 1966 we took a survey in Britain on the attitudes of women toward abortion and on their personal experiences with abortion. This was part of a campaign to change the law in Great Britain. The Abortion Law Reform Association commissioned a series of public opinion polls, the results of which were used to great effect. By far the most significant of these national polls was a survey of attitudes of women toward the abortion law, which sought also information about their personal experiences. This was undertaken by National Opinion Poll during the first half of 1966 when the House of Lords was discussing a private member's bill introduced by Lord Silkin. The results were published immediately before another bill, eventually to pass into law, was introduced in the House of Commons by a young Liberal Member of Parliament, David Steel.

We had no idea at the time whether women who had experienced an induced abortion would reveal their secrets. We, therefore, asked for a pilot run to be undertaken in January 1966. The results were reassuring and National Opinion Poll went ahead in May and June 1966 with the distribution of questionnaires to 3,500 women aged 21 to 65. These questionnaires were handed to the women in sealed envelopes during the course of National Opinion Poll's normal fortnightly surveys of a random sample of electors. The envelope also contained an explanatory letter which stressed the confidential nature of the survey, and, to reassure the women further, they were instructed not to write their names and addresses on the form.

Altogether, 2,132 responses were received. Just under a third of all women who replied thought that the pregnant woman alone should be able to decide whether or not she should have an abortion. The remainder were substantially in favor of consulting only a doctor. Only a third of those replying thought that the father should have the right to prevent a woman from having an abortion.

In answer to questions on the grounds for abortion, 91 per cent of all the women were in favor of abortion being permissible on some ground. If the baby was likely to be born seriously deformed, 85 per cent. If the woman's health would suffer by having the child, 82 per cent. If the mother had been raped, 65 per cent. If the pregnancy was the result of incest, 50 per cent. If she was under sixteen, 36 per cent. And 36 per cent if her living conditions made it undesirable to have a child.

In view of the thalidomide tragedies, it was not surprising that more women were concerned about the risk of fetal abnormality than about their own health. Nor were we surprised to find the extent of support for abortion in cases of rape and incest. But why did only 36 per cent consider living conditions important? They may have been influenced by the publicity then being given to the House of Lords' consideration of a social clause, or by some of the arguments employed by the opponents of such a clause. The form of wording of this clause underwent many changes in Parliament in the effort to find a formula that was generally acceptable. In one stage it referred to women being inadequate as mothers, and I think this is probably what many women took exception to. In the last of the series of National Opinion Polls, undertaken in September 1967, the question was phrased differently, and 64 per cent of women, compared with 67 per cent of men, favored abortion where the pregnant woman is unable to cope with any more children.

In the final draft of the bill, the sexual offense clause was dropped, despite support for it among 82 per cent of both men and women, and the social clause was replaced by an extended health clause which allows the risk to the health of existing children of the family to be considered. This wording probably reflects more nearly the viewpoint of women.

I now come to the abortion experience among the 2,132 women who completed the questionnaire in 1966. Ninety-one had experienced at least one abortion. In 34 percent of all cases of induced abortion, the reason given was, "Too many children, unable to cope with more." This figure rose to 41 per cent among those who admitted having had illegal abortions.

Only a fifth of all the cases said they had severe physical or mental after-effects to the abortion compared with 80 per cent who had mild or no after-effects.

The survey showed that Roman Catholic women are no less likely to have had an abortion than women of other religious convictions, and that in general working-class women were more likely to undergo abortion than middle-class women.

A survey made of our own Family Planning Association members by Madaleine Simms revealed some equally startling results. Here we found that one out of every three of our women members (women comprise nearly two-thirds of our total membership) had sought an abortion at some stage in her life, and one in four had actually obtained one, mostly legally and privately. One male member said he had helped no less than 12 friends to obtain abortions, none of them legal.

SHAINESS: I am surprised by the figure of 50 per cent regarding pregnancy as the result of incest, and also the figure for pregnancy in girls under sixteen. I consider both rather low, and I wonder if this might suggest some sort of punitive attitude.

HOUGHTON: Yes, I'm afraid so.

CALDERONE: May we hear from Dr. Kleegman?

KLEEGMAN: Yes, I have been in private practice for forty-four years, and from the very beginning of my residency at Bellevue Hospital I have been faced every day with the horrendous distinction between the treatment accorded private and ward patients, particularly in the areas of birth control and therapeutic abortion. In my first year of residency, back in 1925, the gynecological service saw the end results of ten illegally induced abortions, of which two were in young girls and eight were in women with four to eight children. In those days before sulfa and penicillin, patients with such severe infections remained in the hospital for months and months, and of those that survived, not one was offered birth control advice. We were not allowed to offer it. What an experience for a young physician who knew that she was trained to save lives and preserve health!

In the first ten years of my residency every woman who came in with an induced abortion was arrested, with a policeman watching her around the clock, and after discharge she had to stand trial. Even up to a year and a half ago, there was very little change as far as the availability of therapeutic abortions to the service cases, and even for the private patient it was not easy to get a therapeutic abortion.

I would say that the greatest need for the majority of private patients and for practically all of the service patients, is for an immediately available counseling resource. The questions these women must be helped to formulate and answer are: What are the alternatives? What are the means by which I can be helped? What support and information will help me reach a wise decision? And, finally, where can I go for a therapeutic abortion?

I feel very strongly that, whether I as a physician do or do not agree with her particular reasons for having an abortion, the ultimate decision should be made by the woman and her husband. But, more important, we must not lose sight of the fact that contraception is the first line of defense, especially for the woman who has had an abortion. If she is exposed to the possibility of pregnancy, then she must be given the means to protect herself against the need of ever having to undergo abortion again.

Since I have enjoyed the security of a wholesome hard-working life with the ability to plan my babies by choice, it is not only as a physician that I look upon this as one of the most serious social injustices—that every woman should not enjoy the very same security and prerogatives. As physicians we see the great differences in mortality rates between legal and illegal abortions. It seems inconceivable that the medical profession should not take definite and strong steps to protect women from the serious health problems relating to illegal abortion. Actually, if this were not in the field of sex, it would have been treated as a health problem from the beginning, and I sincerely hope that this day will come shortly. I may say that there are a few leading physicians who, within the context of the very same New York State law, have greatly broadened the general interpretation of the law by simply taking care of their patients in the light of what they feel to be good health service. I feel very strongly as a physician that the only way we will be able to give honest, just health services to all our women is to have all legal restrictions removed entirely to allow physicians to take care of their patients within the framework of sound medical judgment and practice.

CALDERONE: I was thinking back to the Proceedings of the 1954 Abortion Conference at Arden House, in which there is a list of recommendations agreed upon by all members of the Conference. As I remember it, the important one was the need for a medical center where every unwillingly pregnant woman could go to have her case considered, not brutally or judgmentally, but rationally and confidentially in the light of her total health needs. I remember, too, not very long after, presenting a paper before the American Public Health Association in which, in an effort to try to estimate the case load (of which, as Dr. Dohrenwend indicated, we still have no valid idea), I proposed that abortion requests be made reportable by all physicians. If we had a center on a pilot basis, to which any woman could come and make her request, and then be referred to a physician, we would have a better idea of the case load because abortions that are done are not the total case load. The requests are the real case load, whether they are honored or not. I think this is a serious need. It has not been met.

KLEEGMAN: I would like to call your attention to another book, the Proceedings of the Abortion Conference of 1942, with the same recommendations.

CALDERONE: None of which have been carried out to date except by the Clergymen's Consultation Services in New York City and elsewhere.

MEHLAN: Dr. Kleegman, you mentioned the need for a counseling service for women who request abortion. Are there not committees set up for this purpose?

CALDERONE: Dr. Mehlan means the abortion committees within hospitals.

KLEEGMAN: It is too often done by a group of consultants who pass on a matter of life and death without seeing or examining the patient. What they examine is the information about the patient to arrive at a decision regarding her request for abortion.

KUMMER: I wonder if Dr. Mehlan was not referring to counseling services which are available in Sweden. There a woman with an unwanted pregnancy can go and talk over her problem with a social worker or a physician.

KLEEGMAN: We really haven't had anything like that in this country until recently. It started in New York City with a church-affiliated counseling service, and now others have started in Los Angeles and Philadelphia. This idea is long overdue and should be implemented as widely as possible.

HOUGHTON: Since we have had our law we have started a new organization called the Pregnancy Advisory Service. It started in Birmingham, where about 473 women were interviewed, of whom 450 had pregnancies terminated. They see a social worker and a doctor there. Many of these women were informed about the Service by the press and television. The women were also referred to the Service by social agencies, general practitioners, and the Committee on Doctors.

R. LIDZ: I am a psychiatrist working at Yale in the last two years as a consultant in three projects. One is the "unwed mother" project. One is work in the so-called family-planning clinic. And I have seen 42 women in the hospital for consideration of their requests for abortions. I have brought with me the figures on these 42 women.

There were 11 Negro and 31 white among the 42, 22 married and

20 unmarried. These are all from the general clinic, and in going over my notes I would say that slightly more than 10 per cent had a psychiatric problem before they became pregnant, that is, they were bona fide psychiatric cases. The rest were patients who for some reason or other were desperate because of different sorts of situations or personal reasons—some of them because of their personality difficulties had gotten themselves into trouble. All of these, with two exceptions, deserved an abortion, and I think most of them were approved.

I talked about an hour and a half to each one of these women. I take a history of the woman's background to get a notion about what her adjustment is. I hear about her family or her relations to her boyfriend, or about what is going on in the marriage, and I try to work out how these factors may relate to her need for an abortion. I get a pretty good idea of how she got pregnant, whether it was from a casual contact or in a long-term relationship if not married and so forth, and from all this I bring together enough of the story. In a sense I act as a lawyer to the patient to present her case to the Board and get her abortion approved. I must admit that I am somewhat disliked in this role, because as much as I try to be a therapist and still try to find some sort of way to see into the future, I find these roles difficult to do at the same time. In other words, I do not like having to be both a lawyer and a woman preacher. If the law were removed and I could function in these cases only as a psychiatrist to help the woman, regardless of what her situation is, I feel I would be in a much better position to help her.

The other thing I have to say is that while I would like very much to have all restrictive abortion laws removed, I would like to caution that this is not going to settle all of our problems. It is two different things, to be pregnant and to have the child, and many women are very much mortified by becoming pregnant, but not by having a child. It will take a lot of field work to find out how and when women are going to have trouble and how we can help them avoid it. In this connection I find it helpful to analyze in my own mind what a woman's sexual adjustment is, her measurable or nonmeasurable attitudes toward pregnancy, and her attitudes toward childbirth and toward infertility. The surprising thing is that women say that they do not want more children, yet when they realize that they may be infertile, they always throw up their hands. These are some of the problems, quite aside from the legal one.

CALDERONE: You have skillfully sketched in some of the problems associated with women's sexual lives. Yes, Dr. Stackhouse.

STACKHOUSE: You mentioned two cases in which the decision was that an abortion was not indicated. Could you specify under what conditions these were not recommended, even though desired?

R. LIDZ: The one case was a woman who, although being married a second time and having taken on two children from her husband's previous marriage, became pregnant at a time that she felt was too early. However, in studying the background she handed in I felt that it indicated that this problem was going to be overcome. She had gone to see her gynecologist, who apparently suggested the possibility of abortion, or else at any rate she had the impression that he felt that she should have an abortion. However, I felt that an abortion might be damaging to her, and that if she could have an opportunity to think over the situation she would overcome her objection to having the baby. So I gave her a week's time to think it over and I found out I was right in my appraisal of her situation.

The other was a young girl who I felt would be better off not going through the experience, for psychiatric reasons.

SHAINESS: Dr. Lidz has called attention to the problem of conscious and unconscious attitudes, and she has pointed out the matter of timeliness. Timeliness does not affect a woman's basic attitude, but if a pregnancy is untimely it can be a serious interference. I would be inclined to take the circumstances of the whole family into consideration.

ROEMER: We have spent two days in a very inspiring way recognizing that unwanted pregnancy is a problem of men as well as of women and creates problems in every community. Indeed, it is a problem of society as a whole. To women it has special importance, since they have the responsibility for bearing and rearing the children. Although abortion is not solely a woman's problem, from the point of view of women it is they who must accept and bear the principal consequences of an unwanted pregnancy or find an escape from it.

For this simple biological reason, women, particularly in the developed countries, are coming to regard abortion as a fundamental human right. The struggle for recognition of this right is actually another chapter in the long struggle for the legal, political, and economic rights of women in the family of man. It is a right so fundamental, so personal to women, that its denial nullifies the right to freedom and to security of their person and of their families.

Looking back over the history of the women's rights movement, one sees the efforts, still going on in some countries, to achieve rights in private law—the right of a woman to acquire, dispose of, or inherit property, to enter into contracts, to sue and be sued in her own name, the right of freedom of choice in marriage and of dissolution of marriage, the right of guardianship and custody of children, the right to establish her own domicile and retain her own nationality. In the field of political rights, did the suffragettes dream that in less than a century women would have the vote and be eligible to hold office in 117 countries, and that in only 11 countries would women have no voting rights or be subject to disabilities not imposed on men? Similarly, economic rights to employment, to protection on the job, to equal pay for equal work, and to freedom from discrimination on grounds of sex, are harbingers of recognition of the right to abortion.

In the current scene, recognition of the right of women to birth control is an even more apt precedent for recognition of the right to abortion. Although family planning is justified on grounds of population policy and protection of maternal health and family welfare, implied in all family-planning programs is the right of access to the best contraceptive protection that science can make available. The Supreme Court of the United States in a landmark case struck down a statute denying access to birth control as an unconstitutional invasion of the right of privacy. States and countries most recently France—that had formerly restricted dissemination of birth-control devices and information are lifting these bans. Implied in the position of every world leader who signed the Declaration on Population of Heads of States presented to the United Nations in 1966, and of every country that has adopted an official family-planning policy, is recognition of the right of women to control their reproductive fate and thus to protect the welfare of their families.

This right is inextricably linked to other rights that have been recognized—for example, the right to special protection on the job. Special controls over the hours and working conditions of women have been enacted that are more protective for women than for men workers. Access to abortion would be a further adjustment to the biological vulnerability of women.

Until science has succeeded in producing a perfect contraceptive, political organization is essential to implement the demands of women for freedom from unwanted pregnancies. Legal impediments to abortion can be removed only by political action. The climate of opinion within the medical profession that is antithetical to abortion requires the force of public opinion to effect a change.

For these reasons, I feel that this panel should address itself to political action designed to make abortion freely available to women who want it. We would do well to heed the experience of Great Britain, where abortion law reform was urged more than thirty years ago, but was successful only when public opinion had been mobilized to support it. Women have been voting for centuries for the right to abortion by the very fact of their continued resort to dangerous illegal abortions. It is our task now to achieve proper and safe recognition of this demand and this right more quickly than the struggle for other women's rights would forecast, and I think we may achieve it.

CALDERONE: Are you asking for a motion? If so, I would like to include in it the motion that with every right go certain obligations.

ROEMER: We are carrying out our obligations.

CALDERONE: Not with repeated unwanted pregnancies. The rights and obligations should balance.

R. LIDZ: Yes. I think that I am also for removing the law. I am very much for that, but I do not think that will solve our problems.

CALDERONE: We will have repeaters, for, as Dr. Lidz pointed out, there are many reasons why women get pregnant even though they do not want the child.

KUMMER: I think you are being somewhat punitive. If a woman gets pregnant, and does so repeatedly, this is a sign of an underlying problem.

CALDERONE: Of course, but I was thinking too of the education of young people, not only regarding their rights, but also regarding their obligations.

KLEEGMAN: I do not believe in abortion on demand. I feel very strongly that if a woman asks for an abortion, it is a medical problem, and I do not think physicians should be chaplains. When a woman requests an abortion, then I think it is important that she be given the opportunity to be seen by someone who is trained.

HARDIN: I wonder if you as a physician are facing the responsibilities of physicians to give really adequate medical assistance to women who are having one baby after the other but who cannot get adequate birth information now.

CALDERONE: Dr. Kleegman meant specifically for adequate contraceptive counseling to be part of the granting of any abortion request.

HARDIN: Do we have enough people adequately trained in abortions to do them?

CALDERONE: If not, then we will have to train them. The point I want to make is that we have a picture of many young people marrying today because they know if things do not work out properly, they can get a divorce all too quickly. And to have young people growing up and saying, "Well, we can always get an abortion"—this is what I was driving at. This has already happened in Japan, where multiple abortions are carried out on the same woman. It is too easy.

KUMMER: I still think you are being punitive.

CALDERONE: I accept that possibility!

SHAINESS: In most of the discussions on abortion, there is so little consideration of the woman. It is as if a complex, learned debate goes on while the woman, hanging in air and regarded as nothing more than an encapsulating amniotic sac, is threatened with falling or splitting, but the learned gentlemen seem not to notice, and find no cause for hurry.

An unwanted pregnancy is an act of intercourse "gone wrong"—with the exception of fetal malformation, where the problem occurs after the fact. We might as well punish each coitus as each unwanted pregnancy. Why do we not make a serious effort to penalize the man, when an unwelcome pregnancy occurs?

In only one instance have I, in my private practice, come upon a situation where others were pressuring a woman to have an abortion; and in this case, the out-of-wedlock pregnancy (and result of a one-night relationship) was a defiant act against hypocritical pillar-of-society parents, whose concern was with their own disgrace, while the girl clung to self-destructive defiance—hardly a valid motivation for pregnancy.

I have come to see that the abortion problem is one manifestation of the power struggle between the sexes, with man fearful of and reluctant to surrender power, as is every group which is in command. Woman in the civilized state must contend with an existential dilemma. There are times when her reproductive function is in conflict with her needs as a social creature and with her own rights as a person.

With man, his life is uninvolved after the act of procreation. He is free to continue his life course. If he becomes diseased as a result of coitus, or if he breaks an arm in taking a walk, we ask that he be treated to restore his former state as closely as possible. Nor would we assert that his venereal disease or his broken arm is best for him. But with woman, we insist that she will be damaged physically and psychologically if *her* former state is restored, if her body integrity is restored. I say that if a pregnancy is regarded as an unfelicitous happenstance and is aborted, the abortion restores the former state of integrity, and there is no innate connected sense of damage or guilt, except as the collective social superego, the prevailing attitude, fosters this and confuses the woman. Further, not only is the early fetus not human, but throughout its fetal life it has no cognitive or perceptual capacity.

Simone de Beauvoir points out the lack of reciprocity between the sexes, and asks why women do not dispute male sovereignty. She notes that the Hegelian concept that every consciousness is fundamentally hostile to every other certainly applies to the group consciousness of male and female. She notes that men anxious about their virility are the most hostile to women. (This has been noted by White, Howells, Van Leeuen, and myself.) She feels that in the sexual act, the male regains his integrity at the moment that he transcends it. The female, first violated, then becomes alienated; she is another than herself in pregnancy, and gestation demands heavy sacrifices. She asserts that if the use of violence toward woman through masculine power is prevented, then the male has no superior source of power. Biology, in terms of reproductive difference, is not really the source of woman's inferior position.

De Beauvoir says that woman in early times did not know the pride of creation because it was a *passive* expression of her biologic state and did not involve any project. It was a function, not an activity. In a world in which each was on his own, this was a tremendous handicap.

She notes that most female heroines are oddities—women are on the margin of history. Those women who are rooted in society are also those in subjection to it. But the price of achieving rather than merely functioning is a great one. Women's self-assertiveness is at issue with regard to abortion—in its very nature a refusal to accept the past and the social status quo, and this is a big element in the struggle and the difficulty.

CALDERONE: On the other hand, we need to pay more attention to our men. I think that they are the most neglected people in our society insofar as having an opportunity to think in these areas. Women have far more chance.

CONFERENCE PARTICIPANTS

OLADELE AKINLA, M.B., F.R.C.S., M.R.C.O.G., Lecturer, Department of Obstetrics and Gynecology, College of Medicine, Lagos, Nigeria.

SIMON ALEXANIANTS, M.D., Professor of Obstetrics and Gynecology on leave from Erevan Medical School, Erevan, Armenia, USSR.

JAMES F. ANDREWS, S.T.B., Managing Editor, *National Catholic Reporter*, Kansas City, Missouri.

ROBERTO BACHI, PH.D., Professor of Statistics, Hebrew University, Jerusalem, Israel.

LEONA BAUMGARTNER, M.D., Visiting Professor of Social Medicine, Harvard Medical School, Boston, Massachusetts.

JOSEPH D. BEASLEY, M.D., Professor of Maternal and Child Health and Pediatrics, Tulane University, New Orleans, Louisiana.

BERNARD B. BERELSON, PH.D., President, The Population Council, New York, New York.

MARY CALDERONE, M.D., Executive Director, Sex Information and Education Council of the United States, New York, New York.

DANIEL CALLAHAN, PH.D., Author and Editor, New York, New York.

ANTONIN CERNOCH, M.D., Professor and Director of the Gynecological Clinic of the Postgraduate Medical School, Prague, Czechoslovakia.

SRIPATI CHANDRASEKHAR, PH.D., D.SC.,* Minister for Health, Family Planning and Urban Development, New Delhi, India.

L. P. CHOW, M.D., DR.P.H.,* Director of Taiwan Population Studies Center, Taiwan Provincial Department of Health, Taichung, Taiwan.

*Submitted paper for publication although unable to attend the conference.

PHILIP A. CORFMAN, M.D., Director, Center for Population Research, National Institute of Child Health and Human Development, Department of Health, Education, and Welfare, Bethesda, Maryland.

GEORGE W. CORNER, M.D., LL.D., Executive Officer, American Philosophical Society, Philadelphia, Pennsylvania.

IRVIN M. CUSHNER, M.D., Associate Professor, Department of Gynecology and Obstetrics, The Johns Hopkins University School of Medicine, Baltimore, Maryland.

PETER DIGGORY, M.B., B.S., B.Sc., F.R.C.S., M.R.C.O.G., Consultant Gynecologist, London, England.

BARBARA DOHRENWEND, PH.D., Associate Professor, Department of Psychology, City College of New York.

JOSEPH F. DONCEEL, S.J., PH.D.,* Professor of Philosophy, Fordham University, New York, New York.

LEON EISENBERG, M.D., Professor of Psychiatry, Harvard Medical School, Boston, Massachusetts.

JOHAN W. ELIOT, M.D., Associate Professor, Center for Population Planning, University of Michigan, Ann Arbor, Michigan.

LARS E. ENGSTRÖM, M.D., Assistant Professor, Department of Obstetrics and Gynecology, Karolinska Institute, Stockholm, Sweden.

DAVID M. FELDMAN, Rabbi, Bay Ridge Jewish Center, Brooklyn, New York.

NUSRET H. FISEK, PH.D., Director, Hacettepe University Institute of Population Studies, Ankara, Turkey.

JOSEPH F. FLETCHER, S.T.D., Professor, Social Ethics, The Episcopal Theological School, Cambridge, Massachusetts.

RALPH J. GAMPELL, LL.B., Lecturer in Law, Stanford University, Palo Alto, California.

GUNNAR AF GEIJERSTAM, M.D., Associate Professor, Department of Obstetrics and Gynecology, Karolinska Hospital, Stockholm, Sweden.

B. J. GEORGE, JR., J.D., Associate Director, Practicing Law Institute, New York, New York.

EDWIN M. GOLD, M.D., Clinical Professor, Obstetrics and Gynecology, University of California School of Medicine, San Francisco, California.

*Submitted paper for publication although unable to attend the conference.

DAVID GRANFIELD, LL.B., S.T.D., Professor, Columbus School of Law, The Catholic University of America, Washington, D. C.

ALAN F. GUTTMACHER, M.D., President, Planned Parenthood-World Population, New York, New York.

ROBERT E. HALL, M.D., Associate Professor of Obstetrics and Gynecology, Columbia University College of Physicians and Surgeons, New York.

GARRETT HARDIN, PH.D., Professor, Department of Biological Sciences, University of California, Santa Barbara, California.

LOUIS M. HELLMAN, M.D., Professor and Chairman, Department of Obstetrics and Gynecology, Downstate Medical Center, State University of New York, Brooklyn, New York.

MILTON HELPERN, M.D., Chief Medical Examiner, City of New York.

KURT HIRSCHHORN, M.D., Professor of Pediatrics and Genetics, Mount Sinai School of Medicine, New York, New York.

IMRE HIRSCHLER, M.D.,* Chairman of Department of Obstetrics and Gynecology, Central State Hospital, Budapest, Hungary.

SUNG-BONG HONG, M.D., M.P.H., Professor, Department of Obstetrics and Gynecology, Woo-Sok University Hospital, Seoul, Korea.

VERA HOUGHTON, Chairman, Abortion Law Reform Association, London, England.

PIERRE O. HUBINONT, M.D., PH.D., Professor and Chairman, Gynecological and Obstetrical Clinic, Saint Pierre University Hospital, Brussels, Belgium.

SOPHIA J. KLEEGMAN, M.D., Professor, Obstetrics and Gynecology, New York University Medical Center, New York, New York.

ANDIE L. KNUTSON, PH.D., Professor of Behavioral Sciences, School of Public Health, University of California, Berkeley, California.

JEROME M. KUMMER, M.D., Clinical Professor of Psychiatry, School of Medicine, University of California at Los Angeles.

LAWRENCE LADER, Adjunct Associate Professor of Journalism, New York University, New York, New York.

ROBERT W. LAIDLAW, M.D., Consultant, Department of Psychiatry, The Roosevelt Hospital, New York, New York.

JOHN V. P. LASSOE, JR., Director of Christian Social Relations, Episcopal Diocese of New York.

*Submitted paper for publication although unable to attend the conference.

ZAD LEAVY, LL.B., LL.M., Attorney, Los Angeles, California.

HAROLD LEVENTHAL, LL.B., Judge of the U. S. Court of Appeals for the District of Columbia, Washington, D. C.

RUTH W. LIDZ, M.D., Associate Clinical Professor of Psychiatry, Yale-New Haven Hospital, New Haven, Connecticut.

THEODORE LIDZ, M.D., Professor and Chairman, Department of Psychiatry, Yale University School of Medicine, New Haven, Connecticut.

OCTAVIO RODRIGUES-LIMA, M.D., Professor and Chairman, Department of Obstetrics and Gynecology, School of Maternal Health, Rio de Janeiro, Brazil.

ROY LUCAS, J.D., Research Associate, Twentieth Century Fund, New York, New York.

CURTIS J. LUND, M.D., Professor and Chairman, Department of Obstetrics and Gynecology, School of Medicine and Dentistry, University of Rochester, Rochester, New York.

ISRAEL R. MARGOLIES, PH.D., Rabbi, Beth Am, The People's Temple, New York, New York.

W. PARKER MAULDIN, Director, Demographic Division, The Population Council, New York, New York.

CYRIL C. MEANS, JR., J.D., LL.M., Attorney, New York, New York.

KARL-HEINZ MEHLAN, M.D., DR.SC., M.P.H., Professor and Director, Institute of Hygiene, University of Rostock, German Democratic Republic.

JOHN R. MONTGOMERY, M.D., Assistant Professor of Pediatrics, Baylor University College of Medicine, Houston, Texas.

MINORU MURAMATSU, M.D., DR.P.H., The Institute of Public Health, Tokyo, Japan.

ISAM R. NAZER, F.R.C.S., Medical Advisor, International Planned Parenthood Federation, London, England.

KENNETH R. NISWANDER, M.D., Assistant Professor of Gynecology and Obstetrics, State University of New York at Buffalo.

FRANC NOVAK, M.D., Professor, Gynecological Clinic, University of Ljubljana, Yugoslavia.

WILLIAM B. OBER, M.D., Director of Laboratories, Knickerbocker Hospital, New York, New York.

THOMAS J. O'DONNELL, S.J., PH.L., B.THEOL., Director of Jesuit Residence, Hot Springs, North Carolina.

EDMUND W. OVERSTREET, M.D., Professor and Vice-Chairman, Department of Obstetrics and Gynecology, University of California School of Medicine, San Francisco, California.

HARRIET F. PILPEL, LL.B., Attorney, New York, New York.

WARDELL B. POMEROY, PH.D., Marriage Counselor, New York, New York.

RALPH B. POTTER, JR., TH.D., Assistant Professor of Social Ethics, Harvard University Divinity School, Cambridge, Massachussets.

EUGENE QUAY, LL.B., Attorney, Chicago, Illinois.

CLYDE RANDALL, M.D., Professor, Department of Obstetrics and Gynecology, School of Medicine, State University of New York at Buffalo.

REIMERT T. RAVENHOLT, M.D., Director, Population Service, Office of War on Hunger, Agency for International Development, United States Department of State, Washington, D. C.

MARIANO REQUENA, M.D., M.P.H., Professor and Researcher, Latin American Demographic Center, Santiago, Chile.

RUTH ROEMER, LL.B., Associate Researcher in Health Law, University of California at Los Angeles.

HAROLD ROSEN, PH.D., M.D., Associate Professor of Psychiatry, The Johns Hopkins University, Baltimore, Maryland.

ALICE S. ROSSI, PH.D., Research Associate, Department of Social Relations, The Johns Hopkins University, Baltimore, Maryland.

PHILIP M. SARREL, M.D., Captain, United States Air Force; formerly Instructor in Obstetrics and Gynecology, Yale University School of Medicine, New Haven, Connecticut.

EDWIN M. SCHUR, PH.D., LL.B., Professor and Chairman, Department of Sociology, Tufts University, Medford, Massachusetts.

HERMAN SCHWARTZ, LL.B., Professor of Law, State University of New York at Buffalo.

RICHARD H. SCHWARZ, M.D., Assistant Professor of Obstetrics and Gynecology, University of Pennsylvania School of Medicine, Philadelphia, Pennsylvania.

SHELDON J. SEGAL, PH.D., Director, Bio-Medical Division, The Population Council, New York, New York.

NATALIE SHAINESS, M.D., Lecturer in Psychiatry, Columbia University, College of Physicians and Surgeons, New York, New York.

HARRY L. SHAPIRO, PH.D., Chairman, Department of Anthropology, The American Museum of Natural History, New York, New York.

ROBERT D. SPENCER, M.D.,* Ashland, Pennsylvania.

MAX L. STACKHOUSE, PH.D., Assistant Professor of Christian Ethics, Andover Newton Theological School, Newton Center, Massachusetts.

KRISTER STENDAHL, THEOL.DR., LITT.D., Dean, Harvard Divinity School, Cambridge, Massachusetts.

PERCY E. SUTTON, LL.B., President of the Borough of Manhattan, New York, New York.

CHRISTOPHER TIETZE, M.D., Associate Director, Bio-Medical Division, The Population Council, New York, New York.

VASILIOS G. VALAORAS, M.D., DR.P.H., Professor and Director, Department and Museum of Hygiene and Epidemiology, University of Athens, Greece.

BENJAMIN VIEL, M.D., D.P.H., Professor of Preventive Medicine, University of Chile School of Medicine, Santiago, Chile.

THOMAS A. WASSMER, S.J., PH.D., Professor of Moral Philosophy, Ohio University, Athens, Ohio.

ROBERT B. WHITE, M.D., Professor of Psychiatry, University of Texas Medical Branch, Galveston, Texas.

JOHN W. WHITRIDGE, JR., M.D., Associate Professor of Population and Family Health, The Johns Hopkins University School of Hygiene and Public Health, Baltimore, Maryland.

KENNETH R. WHITTEMORE, Assistant Professor, Department of Economics and Sociology, Agnes Scott College, Decatur, Georgia.

MARTHA YOW, M.D.,* Associate Professor of Pediatrics, Baylor University College of Medicine, Houston, Texas.

*Submitted paper for publication although unable to attend the conference.

CONFERENCE OBSERVERS

JOHN D. ASHER, M.D., Epidemiology Intelligence Service Officer, Family Planning Evaluation Section, National Communicable Disease Center, Atlanta, Georgia.

ROBERT C. BATES, LL.B., Secretary, Rockefeller Brothers Fund, New York, New York.

MILDRED BECK, M.S.W., Chief, Research Support Section, Center for Epidemiologic Studies, National Institute of Health, Bethesda, Maryland.

C. LALOR BURDICK, PH.D., Director, The Lalor Foundation, Wilmington, Delaware.

MICHAEL S. BURNHILL, M.D., Assistant Professor, Department of Obstetrics and Gynecology, Downstate Medical Center, State University of New York, Brooklyn, New York.

RUTH CAMACHO, M.D., Chief, Office of Health and Population Dynamics, Pan American Health Organization, World Health Organization, Washington, D. C.

ROBERT CASTADOT, M.D., M.P.H., Fellow in the Department of Gynecology and Obstetrics, The Johns Hopkins School of Medicine, Baltimore, Maryland.

KATHRYN J. CERATO, Associate Professor and Assistant Chairman, Department of Maternal Health Nursing, State University of New York at Buffalo.

GEORGE C. DENNISTON, M.D., Associate Medical Director, Planned Parenthood-World Population, New York, New York.

MRS. PETER DIGGORY, Child Care Officer, Greater London Council, London, England.

FRANK R. DUNHAM, ESQ., Staff Attorney, Division of Statutory Research and Drafting, Virginia Advisory Legislative Council, Richmond, Virginia.

CAROLA EISENBERG, M.D., Psychiatrist, Staff Member, Health Unit, Massachusetts Institute of Technology, Cambridge, Massachusetts.

FAY ENKE, Trustee, Prynce Hopkins Fund, Santa Barbara, California.

STEPHEN ENKE, PH.D., Trustee, Prynce Hopkins Fund, Santa Barbara, California.

MRS. MARC HUGHES FISHER, Director, Region One, National Council of Negro Women, New York, New York.

STEPHEN FLECK, M.D., Professor of Psychiatry and Public Health, Department of Psychiatry, Yale University School of Medicine, New Haven, Connecticut.

DAVID S. HALL, Senior Health Educator, Bureau of Maternal and Child Health, County of Los Angeles Health Department, Los Angeles, California.

ROBERT A. HATCHER, M.D., Director, Emory University Family Planning Program, Atlanta, Georgia.

CAROLYN HOUSER, Research Assistant, Center for Population Planning, University of Michigan, Ann Arbor, Michigan.

SAGAR C. JAIN, PH.D., Chairman, Population Policy Group, Carolina Population Center, University of North Carolina, Chapel Hill, North Carolina.

SARAH LEWIT, Research Associate, Population Council, New York, New York.

HOWARD W. MITCHELL, M.D., Lecturer, School of Public Health, University of California, Los Angeles, California.

EMILY MOORE, Research Associate, Population Council, Demographic Division, New York, New York.

SIDNEY H. NEWMAN, PH.D., Behavioral Scientist Administrator, Reproduction and Population Research Branch, National Institute of Child Health and Human Development, Bethesda, Maryland.

RONALD W. O'CONNOR, M.D., Chief, Technical Assistance Unit, Family Planning Evaluation, National Communicable Disease Center, Atlanta, Georgia.

H. L. ROSOFSKY, D.D.S., Executive Director, Bruner Foundation, New York, New York.

CARL W. TYLER, JR., M.D., Chief, Family Planning Evaluation, National Communicable Disease Center, Atlanta, Georgia.